MUMBAI'S D

The Uncommon Story of the Common Man

SHOBHA BONDRE

Translated from Marathi by
SHALAKA WALIMBE

Westland Ltd

westland ltd

61, Silverline, Alapakkam Main Road, Maduravoyal, Chennai 600 095

No. 38/10 (New No. 5), Raghava Nagar, New Timber Yard Layout, Bangalore 560 026

23/181, Anand Nagar, Nehru Road, Santacruz East, Mumbai 400 055

93, 1st floor, Sham Lal Road, Daryaganj, New Delhi 110 002

First published in India by OMO Books, Pune 2011

This edition published in India by westland ltd 2013

Copyright © Shobha Bondre 2013

Translation copyright © Shobha Bondre 2011

All rights reserved

10 9 8 7 6 5 4 3 2 1

ISBN: 978-93-82618-23-2

Typeset in Adobe Garamond by SÜRYA, New Delhi

Printed at HT Media Ltd., Noida

Contents

Old code on top of the dabba

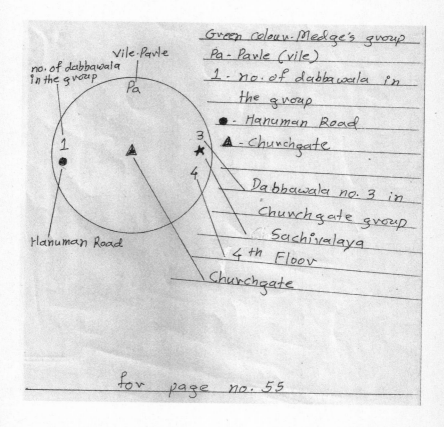

Green colour - Medge's group
Pa - Pavle (vile)
1 - no. of dabbawala in the group
● - Hanuman Road
▲ - Churchgate

Dabbawala no. 3 in Churchgate group
Sachivalaya
4 th Floor
Churchgate

for page no. 55

modern method.

E - Hanuman Road
VLP - Vile-Parle
3 - Churchgate
9 E 12 - Dabbawalo no. 9
delivers dabba on
12th Floor of
Express Towers.

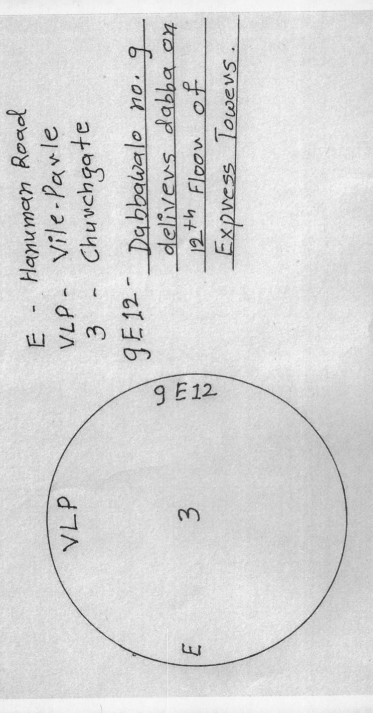

D - Area in Ghatkopar

GH - Ghatkopar

13 - Destination - Grant Road

Dabbawala no. 2 delivers dabba on 9th floor of Panchratna building

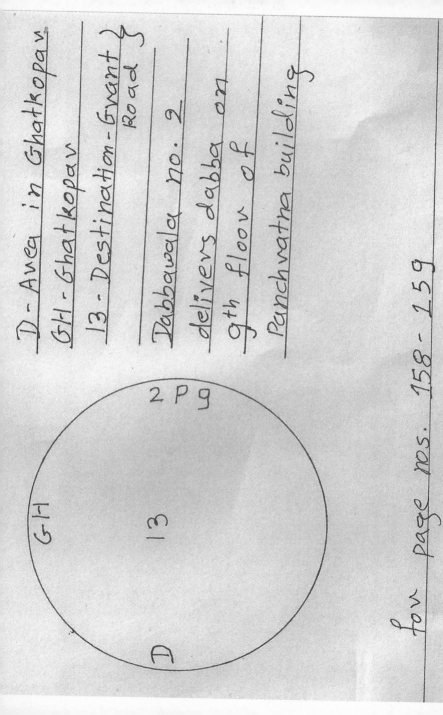

for page nos. 158 - 159

1

London Beckons

As per my daily routine I reached our office in Dadar on that particular day and almost immediately got buried in work. While I was talking to some people, the mobile rang. I took the call. The caller was none other than Mr Jitendra Jain from the British Deputy High Commission—Mumbai.

'Good morning.'

'How are you?'

'Fine, thank you.'

After a brief exchange of pleasantries, Mr Jain got down to business—'How many of the dabbawalas have valid passports ready?'

'Three of us, Mr Gangaram Talekar, Mr Sopanrao Mare and I. Anything in particular?' I enquired.

'Yes, absolutely, get ready and pack your bags, you are to attend a wedding in London. HRH the Prince of Wales has sent the dabbawalas an invitation. He has requested that two people from your organisation be present for the wedding. You must decide who will attend this function.'

It was a bolt out of the blue. Just to double-check, I glanced upon the calendar. It was Friday, the 1st of April 2005. Considering the fact that it was April Fool's Day, I promptly asked Mr Jain, whether he was pulling a fast one on me. He had the heartiest laugh I have ever heard and replied, 'No, no, of course not. If you come by to my office I can show you the invitation letter.'

Later in the day, I reached the office of the British Deputy High Commission and saw the invitation for myself. My heart had never experienced such great joy and pride. It was too good to be true that out of the billion citizens staying in our country—India, two dabbawalas had been accorded the privilege of receiving a special invitation to attend the royal wedding in London!

This recognition and honour was conferred not only on two individuals but more importantly on two dabbawalas of Mumbai. Therefore, it was with great pride that Sopanrao Mare and I, Raghunath Medge, accepted the invitation on behalf of our fraternity of almost five thousand dabbawalas. But in spite of the magnitude of it all, we remained firmly rooted to the ground.

From that moment onwards we had loads to do. The bridegroom was probably taking it easy in his hometown but we were constantly on the move here.

Needless to say, we are accustomed to the daily rat race. My day starts very early in the morning. From home, I head straight to our office in Dadar, then to the Grant Road office, followed by a quick round at Churchgate station and then off to the Cooperative Credit Society office in Andheri. To add to this hectic everyday routine, there were now visits to the British Deputy High Commission, the Air India office, Hotel Tajmahal and several other such places.

We had received the invitation on 1st and the marriage ceremony was scheduled for 8 April. That in effect gave us only six days in hand for preparation. We were worried whether we would be able to manage everything on time but then there is always a ray of hope in such times.

To be extremely honest, we are a bunch of simple, traditional and superstitious people. Earlier, when we had learnt that Prince Charles would be taking his marriage vows on 8 April, a 'no-moon's day', we were very upset as 'no-moon's day' is considered inauspicious by Hindus. Unknown to the world, we dabbawalas had organised a *pooja* and a special sacrificial ceremony on 13 March at the Sanyas Ashram Temple in Mumbai in order to appease the stars and ward off the evil. We had pleaded with the Almighty, 'Lord, though it is the no-moon's day may the Prince's wedding be celebrated without any obstacle.'

The unprecedented death of Pope John Paul II, led to the wedding being postponed by a day as Prince Charles decided to go to Vatican to pay his last respects.

The last-minute postponement gave us one more day in hand for preparation and above all brought with it a sense of relief as the marriage would now be solemnised on the auspicious day of the Hindu New Year. The Lord seemed to have answered our prayers. Reassured by the change in date, we continued with our pre-departure preparations.

The news about the invitation to the royal wedding spread like fire and all the bigwigs in town got their act together. Air India informed us that they would take care of our air tickets. Representatives from Hotel Tajmahal added, 'You must stay in Hotel Tajmahal London. From the time you land in London up to your departure, you shall be our guests.' It was truly overwhelming.

It all seemed like a dream, our passports and visas were ready and just when we thought nothing could go wrong, out of the blue we received a call from Air India office, 'Your tickets are ready. However, when you come to collect them, you will have to make a payment of Rs 9,200 as taxes. As per our rules we can offer you the tickets but cannot waive off the taxes.' This really put us in a fix. Just as Air India had a set of rules, we dabbawalas too followed certain strict rules.

In the past few years I have received several invitations to lectures and felicitation ceremonies. I accept them but have one condition, 'I will certainly come, but please bear my conveyance cost. My organisation should not spend a penny on my travel.'

However this time around the case was different. This was an unusual situation. Some of our organisation members felt, 'This is a unique invitation; one that will only add to the reputation of our organisation and for this reason we must make arrangements for this unforeseen expenditure.'

With the necessary cash in hand, Sopanrao and I reached Air India office. To our surprise several journalists, channel reporters, cameramen and others had gathered there. The staff of Air India was also present to greet us.

Somebody filled out the necessary forms and got them signed by us, some were clicking our photos, others were asking us for interviews. Amidst all the chaos and confusion, representatives from the British Deputy High Commission appeared on the scene and paid the tax amount that we owed to Air India.

All this happened much after the official closing hours of Air India office, yet for once nobody seemed to be too upset about spending extra time in office. The tickets were handed over to us followed by a felicitation ceremony. We were praised and congratulated and were given a memento of an Air India aircraft. It was six in the evening by the time the ceremony came to an end. Everyone seemed truly happy for us and wished us 'good luck and bon voyage'.

When the world outside was taking notice of us and congratulating us, could our families be far behind? Our wives packed our staple diet of *bhakri* and *chutney* for our journey. They also gave us *chivda* for evening snacks. They were in fact worried, 'God alone knows what you will get to eat at Hotel Tajmahal. Our husbands should not go hungry.'

In the meantime, somebody told Sopanrao, 'I have heard that water is very expensive in London.' Promptly Sopanrao's bag was filled up to half of its capacity with bottles of water.

To gift the prince and his bride, we carried with us *til laddoos*, a framed greeting card with a tricolour background and of course a pearl studded *mangalsutra*, (the necklace that Indian ladies wear after the wedding) for our dear sister-in-law, Camilla.

Well, foodstuff and gifts were taken care of. Then came

the question of clothes. What should we wear? Some said, 'If you don't wear a suit you will not be allowed to enter the church.' But I was not convinced, 'So what if they don't let us enter!'

Though I didn't say so, I was sure that after having received such an exceptional invitation nobody would stop us at that point in time.

Finally on 7th April, late in the evening, we boarded the Air India flight to London. I wore a shirt and pant while Sopanrao was in his typical attire of kurta and pyjama.

2

Champagne and Peanut Chutney!

'We will be landing shortly at London's Heathrow airport.'

As I heard the announcement in the aircraft, I started to feel butterflies in my stomach.

This was in fact my second journey abroad. So I knew about things like immigration, customs, etc., but the last time I had gone to Italy, there was a guide with us. This time the two of us were all *alone*!

'Will there be someone to receive us at the airport? Will we understand the Gora Sahib's English?' So many doubts . . .

We got out of the plane and stood stock-still. I was seeing such a huge airport for the first time in my life! But we just followed the crowd and finished all the formalities. As we came out through the customs, we saw an Indian fellow with a placard bearing our names.

'Oof,' we heaved a sigh of relief and followed him.

By the time we sat in the car that had been sent for us by

the hotel, we were absolutely frozen. So much so that even after reaching the hotel, my teeth were chattering. It was just about five or five thirty in the evening, but it was already quite dark.

I said to myself, 'My God! Is this what London weather is like? Such biting cold even in the month of April! Such a cloudy sky! God knows how we are going to bear it!'

The manager of Hotel Tajmahal, Mr Ranjit Philipose, welcomed us with a smile. 'How was your journey? Are you feeling tired?' and then suddenly he noticed our clothes and enquired, 'Have you not brought any sweaters or warm clothes?'

We shook our heads mutely.

He continued, 'It really is very cold here. It even snowed yesterday. You will not be able to survive without warm clothes. Come on. We will go shopping and buy you some winter wear. It will be a gift full of "warm" wishes from our hotel!'

We felt embarrassed. I said, 'No, no! That will not be necessary, sir.'

But he refused to take no for an answer. He escorted us once again to the same car and took us to one of the big shops in London.

He bought us two sweaters and then started insisting that we buy a suit each. Finally I bought one for 120 pounds. Sopanbhau said to me, 'I don't want a suit. I will wear the jacket you have brought with you from Mumbai, if I need to.'

When we got back to the hotel, I thanked Mr Philipose

and told him, 'Sir, I bought the suit because you insisted, but I will leave it here before returning to Mumbai. What will I do with it there?'

Mr Philipose laughed and said, 'We will talk about that later. Why don't you start using the suit from tomorrow?'

Then he escorted us himself to our room. I don't know if it was because we were there for a VIP wedding, but Hotel Tajmahal was really treating us like kings.

'Please come in.' Mr Philipose said, 'We have reserved this VIP suite especially for you.

When we entered, it really seemed like a king's palace to us.

When we said as much to Mr Philipose, he smiled and said, 'That is absolutely correct. It is in fact the maharajas of today who stay in this suite. Top politicians, super-rich industrialists, famous actors and actresses . . . Mr Lal Krishna Advani was staying here before you. Even now, do you know who is staying in the suite next to yours? It is Mr Amitabh Bachchan!'

'You mean to say that we are Amitabh Bachchan's neighbours!' We hadn't imagined that this would be possible even in our wildest dreams. I said, 'He too must have come here for the wedding.'

Mr Philipose shook his head, 'No no. He has not been invited for Prince Charles's wedding.' I was too overwhelmed to be surprised. I decided to take things as they came.

There was no time to rest. The London press and television reporters would be coming to the hotel to interview us.

We took a wash, changed our clothes and ate a little. Not

only was the food completely vegetarian and Indian, but the waiter who served us even spoke Hindi. The interpreter who was going to interpret for us at the Press Conference was also fluent in both English and Hindi. Thanks to all this, we hardly felt we were in a 'foreign' country.

We had hardly finished our lunch when we were surrounded by the press people.

The first question everyone asked us was, 'What do you think of London?'

I replied, 'It feels like I am at my aunt's house. The house might be different from ours but it has the love and warmth of my mother. What I mean to say is that we feel comfortable and at home like we do in Mumbai.'

From that moment onwards we were deluged with questions. Flash bulbs were popping, cameras were being clicked. Everyone was curious, 'Why does Prince Charles like you so much?'

I replied with a lot of examples from the Ramayana and Mahabharata—the affection between Lord Rama and his younger brother Bharata; the meeting between Lord Krishna and his poor friend Sudama, how Krishna loves Sudama's simple and humble offering of puffed rice; the devotion of Shabari who tastes each berry to check its sweetness before offering it to Lord Rama . . . and so on. I really wonder how much they understood of all that!

I had tried to make them see the unique relationship that we dabbawalas (tiffin carriers) from Mumbai shared with Prince Charles.

I also told them, 'Sudama wanted to ask Lord Krishna for

a favour. It is something else that finally he couldn't bring himself to ask Krishna for help. But, in fact, we dabbawalas do not want anything from Prince Charles apart from his goodwill and best wishes. We have come here today to express our gratitude and love for him. It was only after Prince Charles came to meet us in Mumbai that we were noticed not just by the rest of the world but by India as well.'

Our jaws were aching after talking so much but the flow of questions just wouldn't stop. Finally, our interpreter took matters into his hands and announced, 'Ladies and gentlemen, we will stop here. Our guests have to get up early tomorrow to attend Prince Charles's wedding and they have a long day ahead of them.'

We got up early on Saturday morning. I wore the suit I had bought in London, while Sopanbhau wore his traditional kurta-pyjama (a long shirt with baggy pants) with my jacket. Finally, we wore the white Gandhi cap, a trademark of the dabbawalas, without which our costume wouldn't have been complete. Some may say, 'A Gandhi cap with a suit! What a combination! The two don't go well together at all.'

Well, my reply to them would be, 'If the royal wedding and we dabbawalas from Mumbai can go well together, I don't see what is wrong with wearing a Gandhi cap with a suit!'

At eight o'clock sharp, Mr Oliver Brend came to pick us up. Mr Brend was an official of the Prince of Wales Charitable Foundation. First, he took us to the Buckingham Palace, the London residence of Queen Elizabeth.

From there, we went in a luxurious 28-seat bus to the

Windsor palace along with some other members of the royal household. Here, we were to attend the ceremony in the chapel and bless the royal couple.

The organisation was excellent. Every chair had a number and a name attached to it. 750 guests from all over the world had been invited for the ceremony, but there was no confusion or disorder. Everyone was escorted to his or her seat.

Sopanbhau and I were both a little overwhelmed but of course very happy to be there. We were dazzled by the grand sight and felt as if we were in God Indra's (the King of the Gods) court!

The glitter and the glamour, the huge chandeliers, the well-dressed gentlemen and the women dripping with diamonds and other jewels left us speechless!

In fact, we had been almost silent since we left the hotel this morning. We didn't have an option! There was no interpreter with us today and for the life of us we couldn't make sense of all the 'Yes-Phess' going on around us.

So there we were, sitting quietly, when we heard a voice asking us from the seat next to ours, 'May I help you?'

We turned our head and saw an Indian lady, dressed in Indian clothes, smiling at us. She introduced herself. She was none other than the maharani of Jaipur, Maharani Padmini Devi! We too introduced ourselves. She was very kind and assured us, 'You will not have a problem of language! I will interpret for you!' Once again, we were speechless! There were no words to express our thanks!

Even after a long time, there was still no sign of the royal couple. When we asked Padmini Devi the reason, she informed us that the wedding had actually taken place at Guildhall, the riverside royal weekend retreat, 50 kms from London. There were only about 25 guests at that function, including their children from their previous marriages and some very close relatives. Even Queen Elizabeth was not present for that ceremony.

Queen Elizabeth and Prince Philip would be coming to the St George Chapel, where we guests were assembled. There were thousands of people lining the road. Everyone was waiting for the royal couple to arrive.

At last the wait was over. The newly-wedded couple, Prince Charles and Camilla entered the chapel.

The ceremony began. The royal priest started reciting the prayers. Everyone stood up. They had their prayer books open and were reading from them. We too had the prayer books in our hand. We opened them and lip-synched the prayers, pretending to read everything that was written there.

During the Maharashtrian wedding ceremony, we distribute among the guests, coloured rice grains, which we shower on the married couple, similarly, here, we had been given dried rose petals. After the prayers were over, everyone showered the royal couple with the rose petals. We too flung the rose petals in the general direction of Prince Charles.

The wedding feast began in style, with the popping of a champagne bottle, and the fizz being sprayed everywhere. We too sipped a little champagne along with all the other guests.

As for the wedding feast itself! What a spread! Just looking at all the varied dishes was enough to make us feel full.

Though, of course, we didn't know the name of a single dish or what it was made of! We looked around us and just did what the other people were doing.

Prince Charles and his bride Camilla were now greeting their guests. They were smiling and talking to them. We stood out because of our Gandhi caps! They noticed us and started coming in our direction. I immediately took a quick look at my right palm. Do you know why? In the morning, before leaving the hotel, I had written down a sentence there, in English, in ball-point pen, 'We wish you a very happy married life!' There wasn't going to be an interpreter with us at the ceremony and I was not sure I would remember the whole sentence correctly at the last moment! I have never cheated during exams but this time I had taken care to see that I don't fail!

I kept on repeating the sentence in my mind and the moment I saw Prince Charles in front of me, I quickly repeated it. Prince Charles smiled and said, 'Thank you.' He then shook my hand and started talking to me as easily as he would talk to a friend, 'We received the gift you sent from Mumbai two weeks ago. We liked the turban and the green sari for Camilla very much. And most importantly, we appreciate the sentiments behind the gift. I will always treasure your gifts as a fond memory of you. Please do say hello on my behalf to all the dabbawalas in Mumbai. Tell them I remember them.'

When Padmini Devi translated Prince Charles's words into Hindi, I had tears in my eyes. My throat felt constricted with emotion and I couldn't utter a single word. Madame

Camilla arrived at that moment. Prince Charles introduced us to her. She too smiled and said, 'I liked your gift. Thank you very much.' We just nodded our heads in reply.

Now that we had met the royal couple, we could have left. But Padmini Devi said, 'Come, I will present you to Queen Elizabeth, you can talk to her for a couple of minutes.'

A couple of minutes! It was well over five minutes and the queen was still talking to us. She asked us a lot of questions. Padmini Devi, our interpreter for the day, answered the questions on our behalf. I felt as if all this was a dream and naturally I didn't want this dream to ever end!

As the feast came to an end, Prince Charles and Camilla left for their honeymoon. All the guests came outside to wave them goodbye. Charles and Camilla got into a beautifully decorated, luxurious car on which were written the words . . . C + C = love. I think it meant that Charles and Camilla should live happily ever after.

Padmini Devi whispered in my ear, 'This was the children's idea!' I was amused that children too could have any ideas about their parents' wedding and offer them their best wishes! But then at the same time, I also realised and appreciated the openness of this country's culture.

After having waved goodbye to Charles and Camilla, we returned to our hotel.

The next day was Sunday. We got up late. We decided that we would have breakfast and go out to see London. Just then the phone rang. When I picked it up, I was given the 'good?' news: 'The restaurant will be closed today so we will not be able to provide food for you. We apologise for the inconvenience.'

I was confused. How can the restaurant be closed? But then I said that it might be possible. The rules are different in every country.

Sopanbhau was already awake. When I repeated the message to him, he said,

'No problem. We have our *bhakri* and *chutney* with us. We will eat that and go out.'

We both had a bath and then we opened our tiffin boxes and started eating. I tell you, the taste of that *bhakri* and *chutney* was out of this world!

When we had a sip of water, the London water seemed absolutely tasteless! So I told Sopanbhau, 'Take out that bottle of water you packed in your bag in Mumbai. We have to have "Indian" water with our traditional Indian breakfast!'

We were in the middle of our breakfast, when our Hindi-speaking waiter knocked and entered. He looked at us in surprise and asked, 'What are you eating?'

I told him what we were eating and why and then asked him, 'Would you like to taste it?'

He was embarrassed and he said no initially. However we insisted and he then had a bite of the *bhakri* and *chutney*. He nodded his head in appreciation and said, 'This is delicious! Please could I have some more?'

After we had finished this 'royal' meal, the waiter asked us, 'Sir, could you please give me the recipe for that chutney? I will give it to the hotel chef and ask him to make exactly the same chutney.'

Can you believe it? Our traditional peanut chutney had been appreciated in no less than a five-star hotel in London.

The phone rang once again. I picked up the receiver and said, 'Hello, Good morning.'

It was Mr Philipose, 'And a very good morning to you too. I have called up on behalf of the hotel to request you to extend your stay by another two days. You can do some sightseeing before you leave.'

'But Sir, our tickets are booked for tonight.'

Mr Philipose laughed and replied, 'Please do not worry about that. I will contact Air India and get your tickets confirmed for two days later. OK?'

Now I gave Sopanbhau this really good news. He didn't say a word and just looked at me. I knew exactly what he was feeling. How the days had changed!

Until three or four years ago, everyone used to make fun of us. Some would call us, 'ghati' (uncouth) while others would ridicule us and call us, 'Mama' (simpleton).

Today however, there seemed to be a golden halo around our head. Three years ago, Prince Charles came to meet us at the railway station at Churchgate and he appreciated our work and gave us respect and admiration.

We were still the same. But the people's attitude towards us had changed.

I have already narrated the wedding story but there are a few more amusing incidents to tell.

Since we had now got two days to see London, we visited all the places that tourists usually visit ... many museums, the parks that stretch for miles on end, palaces, huge shops and South Hall, what you could call the little India in London.

However, we didn't do even one penny worth of shopping. There were two reasons for this: First, we were not here on business or to make money. We were here as somebody's guest. We had seen London and that was more than enough for us. Why waste money on shopping?

The second reason was that we could get everything we needed, we wanted in Mumbai itself. So there was no need to buy things only to show off that we had got them from London.

Before we left, we had to meet the Press reporters once more. We were being asked the same questions again. Then someone asked, 'When will you come back next?'

I replied, 'If Prince Charles decides to get married a third time, we will definitely come to wish him.' There was a burst of laughter and then finally everyone took our leave.

A final interesting anecdote: Before leaving Mumbai, we had changed Rs 10,000 into 180 British Sterling pounds, which we had kept with us in case of an emergency. After we returned to Mumbai, I went to the exchange bureau and gave back the 180 pounds. Instead of the Rs 10,000 that I was expecting, I got only Rs 9,500. I wondered if the pound rate had gone down so much in a few days. I then learnt that the exchange bureaus earned during both the buying and selling transactions. When you buy foreign currency, the rupee's value is lower but if you sell that foreign currency even at the next moment, you still get less money for the foreign currency.

Anyway, thanks to this trip abroad, we spent Rs 500 and received this piece of information. And that bit of knowledge is the only thing we 'bought' on this trip!

3

'NMTBSA' an Impressive Organisation

There is one clarification I would like to make at the outset.

'Mumbaicha Dabbawala' is the story of the dabbawalas (tiffin carriers) of Mumbai.

Some parts of this story will be related in the first person, from the perspective of the hero of this story, Mr Raghunath Medge, and sometimes it will be me, the author, who will take on the role of the narrator. I feel sure that this dual-edged narrative will give the reader a comprehensive view of the amazing world of the dabbawalas.

So, the story of the 'Nutan Mumbai Tiffin Box Suppliers' Association' or in other words, the story of the dabbawalas of Mumbai is more than 100 years old.

This story dates back to the time when Mumbai was made up of seven islands and only around three or four villages, when the railway network had not yet formed its complex web, when India was still governed by the British: at that time, in 1890, one Mahadu Havji Bacche came to Mumbai to earn a living. He began carrying the tiffin boxes and became the first 'dabbawala' of Mumbai.

However, the incredible fact is that we came to know about him and the dabbawalas and their incredible efficiency only a few years ago.

Prince Charles visited India in November 2003. He made it a point to meet the dabbawalas. He was eager to know more about their work and he praised their dedication and efficiency.

No sooner had Prince Charles met the dabbawalas, than they became the focus of media attention. All the important newspapers in Mumbai carried prominent articles about them on the front page, programmes about them were aired on all the major television channels and all of a sudden, they caught the attention not only of the Indian public but even of the people of Mumbai. There was only one question on everyone's lips, 'Who are these incredible dabbawalas?'

This is a typical Indian characteristic, isn't it? If anything Indian is lauded in the West, only then do we realise its significance, whether it relates to Ayurveda, Yoga or breast-feeding! When we see aloe vera as an ingredient in expensive imported cosmetic products, we are impressed and it takes a while to figure out that it is a shrub that is very commonly found in our country and which we ignored until recently.

Until recently, the dabbawalas of Mumbai were ignored and neglected like the cactus or the aloe vera shrub. It is only when Prince Charles called them 'amazing!' that we recognised the true worth and admirable achievements of the dabbawalas of 'NMTBSA'.

It all started with the world famous *Forbes* business magazine bestowing the prestigious 'Six Sigma Plus' performance rating for the precision of the dabbawalas of Mumbai.

This placed them in the league of giant companies such as Motorola and GE.

Once they had been acknowledged by *Forbes* magazine, the rest of the media was quick to follow suit. The *Time* weekly published an article titled, 'Dabbawalas of Bombay'. The reputed BBC made a film on them. Prince Charles watched this film on BBC and was enthralled. It aroused his curiosity about this incredible organisation.

The illiterate dabbawalas accurately interpret the symbols marked on the tiffin boxes; these tiffin boxes are then transported across the vast city of Mumbai to unerringly reach the correct person; during this 60-70 kms journey these tiffins are handled by three or four dabbawalas and change trains a couple of times. In spite of this complex procedure it is almost impossible that the tiffin box reaches the wrong person. There occurs an error once in every 600,000 transactions! This should definitely rank as the eighth wonder of the world!

The recognition given by the *Forbes* magazine to the dabbawalas was only the beginning of a long list of awards and commendations!

- 'Best Time Management'
- An entry in the *Guiness Book of World Records*
- Overwhelming praise in *Ripley's 'Believe it or not'*

- Awards from the IIM (Indian Institute of Management) and other Indian institutions of repute
- One subject of research in the Faculty of Journalism at the California University is 'The Dabbawalas of Mumbai'
- Several management students in India prepare projects and case studies on the dabbawalas of Mumbai
- Popular international and national television channels such as BBC, CNN, Zee news, Star News, NDTV have aired films on dabbawalas and interviewed them.

In short, Mumbai's dabbawalas are the 'happening' news these days!

'What is the secret of this amazing success story? Who can take the credit for it?'

I started out with these same questions that arise first in the common man's mind whenever he hears about the dabbawalas.

I decided to begin my quest by meeting Mr Raghunath Medge, the president of the NMTBSA. He is the centre of attraction these days and everyone seems to acknowledge him as the inspiration behind the success story of the dabbawalas.

I did not have any difficulty in finding Mr Medge's mobile number. Without further ado, I called him.

After the customary greetings were over, I told him the reason why I was calling.

'I would like to write a book on the dabbawalas. When could we meet?'

'Why not today?' was the unexpected reply.

To tell you the truth I am accustomed to working at a leisurely pace. But now that I was dealing with the super-efficient dabbawalas I had no choice and I agreed to meet him the very same day.

Mr Medge said, 'All right then. Please come to our office in Andheri, a suburb of Mumbai, at four o'clock. This is the address: Deccan Maval Pathapedi, Raghunath Pathak Chawl, Room number 3, Sambhaji Nagar, Sahar Road, Andheri (East). It is below the Andheri fly-over, opposite Vijaynagar Colony, next to Kanifnath Juice Centre . . . Will you be able to find or do I need to give you any further directions?'

Actually I was dazed with all these rapid-fire directions, but I said, 'Yes. I have understood. I will be there at four o'clock.'

I had just had a first-hand experience of the amazing efficiency of the dabbawalas and I was beginning to understand the reason for their phenomenal success.

4

From 'Bhonawala' to 'Dabbawala'

After speaking to Mr Medge and several other dabbawalas, I managed to gather a lot of information about the growth of their profession.

Mahadu Bacche came to Mumbai in 1890. He started looking for work. He began by hauling sacks of provisions for grocers, unloading the cargo off ships and doing other menial jobs. He was earning a little bit of money but he was always on the lookout for fresh opportunities.

There were very few restaurants in Mumbai in those days and certainly no fast-food outlets. There were only a few Sindhi and Christian housewives who used to provide home-cooked food.

Mahadu Bacche had a novel idea. He started transporting lunch boxes to the government offices in the Fort area of Mumbai. Thanks to him, many government employees could now enjoy food, freshly cooked at their home, which was delivered to them on time for lunch.

Bacche was an enterprising soul. He recognised the potential of this new-found venture and saw the possibilities of growth it offered. So he promptly wrote to his hometown in the district of Maval and called other young men who were in search of employment, to Mumbai.

The Maval district in the western region of Maharashtra comprises of villages such as Junnar, Rajguru Nagar, Sangamner, Akola, Mulshi and Ambegaon. This is a rocky and mountainous land. Agriculture is the only means of livelihood in this area. However, the scope for agriculture is limited on account of the rocky terrain and it is totally dependant on rain water.

Many young men responded to Mahadu Bacche's call and came to Mumbai. These hardy young men who were once respected and feared as they were the brave soldiers of the warrior king Shivaji, now became the dabbawalas of Mumbai.

These men with surnames such as Shelar, Pawar, Jadhav, Shinde, Kadam, Pingle were now conferred with another name by the Parsi housewives: they were called 'Bhonawalas' which means 'the one who carries lunch' in Gujarati.

The 'Bhonawalas' used to live in the Girgaum area which lay just outside the Fort area and they used to walk for miles to transport the tiffin boxes. These men who had grown up in the rough mountainous regions possessed inherent strength and the courage and persistence of their ancestors. Moreover, they were used to a life of hard labour and that is the reason these Maval youth could survive in this tough profession right up to the present times.

In the early years of the 20th century, Raghunath Medge's

father's uncle came to Mumbai. He too followed the stream of Maval youth who were making their way to Mumbai in search of a better future and became a dabbawala.

The dabbawalas were growing rapidly in number. Mumbai too was progressing at an amazing pace. As the industries grew, the islands forming Mumbai were joined and the city spread horizontally and vertically. There was never a dearth of work for the dabbawalas. The work involved tough physical labour but one was assured of a reasonable income.

Gradually, the railway network developed in Mumbai. The dabbawalas started using the railways for transporting the tiffin boxes and thus increased the area they covered. They put in to place a system which assured the timely delivery of tiffin boxes anywhere from Virar or Vasai to Churchgate and from Kalyan to VT.

Handcarts and bicycles started being used and instead of the traditional round basket, long rectangular crates were introduced, which could transport 30 to 35 tiffin boxes at a time.

To a large extent, the credit for their efficient management system goes to the ideas of those initial dabbawalas like Mahadu Bacche. From the very beginning this business was always run with precision, coordination and discipline.

Nowhere in the world do we see such a perfect example of the implementation of the relay system. Where one dabbawala can manage to transport not more than 25 to 30 tiffin boxes, a team of 20 dabbawalas working in perfect coordination can easily deliver 700-800 tiffin boxes between them!

It was due to these innovative ideas that the dabbawalas'

business grew as rapidly as any industrial venture. Today there are five thousand dabbawalas. They account for the transportation of two lakh tiffin boxes between them!

Every dabbawala earns about Rs 5,000 to Rs 6,000 and the annual turnover of their organisation is approximately Rs 75 crores.

In the olden days all these men were totally illiterate. Today most of them can read and write but not a single dabbawala has studied beyond the seventh or eighth grade. The only exception is Mr Raghunath Medge. He is a graduate in the arts faculty, (BA), and has also studied a little bit of law.

Even though these illiterate people come from the backward regions of Maharashtra, they have always run their organisation with strict discipline and total adherence to its rules and regulations. The NMTBSA became a registered organisation only in the year 1956. However, its rules and regulations were defined from its very inception.

Another important characteristic is the chain-like system of transport that they follow. Over the years, they have managed to perfect this relay system and its time-work-speed ratio. 'Work is God' has always been their motto and it is undoubtedly a key factor in their success.

In 1940, Raghunath Medge's father, Dhondiba Medge accepted his uncle's invitation to come to Mumbai and became a dabbawala. In those days, the dabbawalas used to share a room in areas like Khetwadi, Grant Road and Dadar. In fact, some of them, at the beginning of their career, even lived on the pavement. Luckily, the weather in Mumbai is so mild that apart from the monsoon season, it is quite bearable and in fact sometimes even more airy, dwelling on the pavement. The dabbawalas would take a bath at the community water tap in the morning and begin their day's work. At night, after eating in a roadside eatery, they would spread their bedding on the pavement and go to sleep.

Dhondiba Medge started out on wages of Rs 8. Of this, Re 1 was spent on boarding, Rs 2 was for other miscellaneous expenditure and Rs 5 was to be kept aside to be sent back home to his family in the village or sometimes for some unexpected expense.

During the rainy season, many dabbawalas would go back to their villages to help with the sowing of crops. However, there were many who stayed in Mumbai. When it rained heavily, it became impossible to sleep on the pavements. At times like these, the dabbawalas would go to the nearby theatre where the local dance form 'tamasha' was performed and book a seat at the back of the auditorium. In fact, this was not to see the performance but to get a good night's sleep. 'Were the "tamasha" theatres being used for this purpose by any one else apart from the dabbawalas?' This could perhaps be the new subject of research for a case study!

Once the dabbawalas had saved enough money, they would rent a room, in a group of course! One room was shared by 15 to 20 dabbawalas. Each person had very meagre possessions: a bedding roll and an extra pair of clothes in a small metal trunk, that is all!

Dhondiba realised that by living frugally and spending with caution, one could manage to save some money. And so, this man who had studied only up to the fourth grade, but who was worldly-wise, soon started to improve his lot.

Dhondiba provided for his four brothers and their families who lived in his village, 35 or 40 members in all. He started buying agricultural land whenever he could save money. He came from the village of 'Aavadar' but since this was not a very developed region, he also bought land in other areas like 'Kadus'.

He also bought a small room in a chawl for Rs 250 in the suburb of Vile Parle. Gradually, he became the 'mukadam' or supervisor of seven tiffin boxes. He started doing other work for the Dabbawalas' Association.

Dhondiba, with his charismatic personality and leadership qualities, became the president of the association. Then, he decided to contest the election from his village on a Jan Sangh party ticket. His election symbol was the lamp. However, he lost to the Congress party and thus, the 'lamp' of his political aspirations was snuffed out before it could even be lit.

In spite of the election debacle, Dhondiba's popularity in the villages of Maval did not diminish in any way.

This man, who had gone to Mumbai 25 or 30 years ago with nothing to call his own and had started out by living on the pavement, was today responsible for the livelihood of hundreds of people. He had helped many youth from his village to find work. Dhondiba now owned a lot of property in the village, a flat of his own in a good appartment building in Mumbai and was at the top of the ladder of his profession. Everyone in the Maval region looked upon him as their idol and yearned to be like him.

In Mumbai, the initial 'bhonawala' had by now come to be known as the 'dabbawala'. Some also called him 'tiffinwala'. But what was important is not the appellation but the work that they were doing. They provided food to hundreds of thousands of people in Mumbai and did their job to perfection. This lifeline of the office-goers was functioning efficiently because of its hard working members but at the same time it is necessary to make a special mention of one of its most innovative and dedicated member, Dhondiba Medge.

5

Learning the 'ABCD' of English and of Business

It was the year 1974. I was on my way to school to collect my result of the matriculation examination. My mother gave me a Rs 20 note and said, 'Raghu, while coming back, get some "pedhas" (sweets) to offer God.'

I was surprised, 'Rs 20 worth of pedhas for God?'

Aai (that is what I call my mother) started laughing. 'No silly, two pedhas are enough for God. The rest is for everyone else who comes to our house to wish you.'

She was right. Only two people, my mother and I, were staying in our house in the village of Kadus, but with the servants and the guests who came very often from our village, it amounted to a big number.

I pocketed the money and set off for school. There was quite a huge crowd of students and their parents, all eager to know the result. When I got the result, I glanced at it and couldn't believe my eyes.

I had scored 74 per cent marks but I had failed!

Failed? Yes. I had done well in all the subjects but I had failed in English. That is why Raghunath Medge had failed in the exam! I crumpled the piece of paper in my hand and started back home. My head was reeling.

Aai must be ready to greet me with the traditional 'aarti', Baba (father) too must be waiting impatiently for my result in Mumbai. It had already been decided that I will go to Mumbai after the result and take admission in 'Parla College' in Vile Parle. All of a sudden, my knees gave way. I supported myself against a tree and sat down. I was dazed.

It was not only my parents who were waiting impatiently for my result. It was the entire Medge clan! I was the first member of the Medge family who had always done well in school, had never failed, had managed to reach this far in studies and who dreamed of going to college!

Tears were streaming down my face but at the same time there was the glimmer of a smile. Now I would also be the first Medge to have failed in the matric exam because ironically I was the only one who had reached up to that level!

I wiped my tears on my shirt sleeve. I was still sitting under the tree, lost in thought, looking at the boys who were passing. Some of them were overjoyed that they had passed and others who like me had failed were walking with their heads bowed, deeply dejected.

I sat there till almost everyone had gone and then went back home. Aai had not gone to the fields today. She was waiting for me. As soon as she saw me, she ran towards me and asked, 'What happened, my son?' I hung my head in shame and murmured, 'Failed with a first class!'

She couldn't understand, 'First class and still failed?'

I explained about my miserable marks in English.

Aai must have been disappointed too but she didn't show it, 'Don't worry. It is all right.'

When I heard these words I couldn't help myself and I burst into tears.

Whenever something terrible happens, we are stunned in the beginning but after the initial shock, we realise that we have to find a way out of the situation.

Before going to sleep that night, I told my mother, 'I will not go to Mumbai now. I will stay here and help you with the farming.'

Aai patted me lovingly on my head, 'Don't be silly, child. Just because you failed once, that doesn't mean it is the end of the world. Nothing doing! You will go to Mumbai as decided. Baba will see what is to be done.'

I went to Mumbai. When I reached home and touched my father's feet, I started crying once again. With trembling hands, I gave him the result. Baba looked at it carefully and then patted me reassuringly on the back, 'Don't worry. The only problem is in English. Otherwise, you have done so well in all the other subjects!'

I was feeling much better already.

Baba found a solution to the problem in a minute! 'Raghunath, you will stay here now. Take admission in Pinge's Classes. They will work on your English. Appear for the exam again in October and you will pass. See, it is as easy as that!'

So, instead of college, I now started going to Pinge's Classes. As for crying over my failure, there was no time for that. That is a characteristic and also a quality of the city of Mumbai. Nobody ever has a moment to spare here. So, like the other 'Mumbaikars' (people of Mumbai), I too was caught up in a whirlwind routine.

I was so busy, that I didn't notice how the days whizzed past! Going from Vile Parle to Dadar, to attend Pinge's Classes, starting once again with the English alphabet and relearning the ABCD of the language, dropping off my younger sister to school on the bicycle, keeping an account of the tiffin boxes, at time even picking up or delivering the tiffin boxes when needed . . . The list of things to do was endless!

I had visited Mumbai several times during the vacations. But now that I was living here as a 'Mumbaikar', and also working as a dabbawala, I gradually started realising the greatness of my father, Dhondiba Medge.

Baba was the 'mukadam' or chief of the dabbawalas in Vile Parle. In those days, there used to be a mukadam in charge of each area. He was almost the king of that area. To add to it all, my father was also the president of the Nutan Mumbai Tiffin Box Suppliers' Association. So, he was, in fact, the king of kings!

On the one hand, he was a prominent personality among the dabbawalas and at the same time, he was also a highly respected person in Vile Parle. The majority of the people in

Vile Parle, in those days, were educated, middle-class Maharashtrians, a few rich Gujarati businessmen and some local Christians who lived near us.

Actually, my father didn't belong to any of these groups. He was from a small village in Maval, he had studied only up to the fourth grade and his profession was carrying tiffin boxes. But his tough life in Mumbai had made him street-smart and wise and he got along well with all these people.

Well-to-do shop owners like Nandu Kulkarni, rich industrialists like Navinbhai Thakkar, Ruia and Rajpuria considered him a close friend. This was because of his frank and generous nature, his crystal-clear conscience and his habit of going out of his way to help people.

Earlier, there was no drama theatre in Vile Parle. The plays were staged in an open field. It was the responsibility of Nandu Kulkarni's Eastern Decorators to build a stage, arrange chairs and erect a makeshift pandal. Once or twice a small fight began during a performance. Nandu Kulkarni only had to call his friend Dhondiba once, and he came running to the rescue with a hundred-strong army of Maval dabbawalas. When the mob saw Dhondiba's imposing figure in his usual dhoti-kurta, with his band of courageous men, nobody dared to continue the fight.

That set the trend for all programmes in Vile Parle and from that time onwards it was always Dhondiba who was in charge of the security.

In addition to this, Dhondiba was always willing to help people get their municipality licences, government clearances, get patients admitted into hospitals and so many other things.

Thanks to his profession of carrying tiffins, he knew so many people, from municipality engineers to government officials, from doctors to top executives in big companies ... they were all his friends.

The incredible fact was that Dhondiba went out of his way to help people without expecting anything in return. No wonder then that people said with pride, 'I know Dhondiba Medge!' There were many who were sure that they could count on Dhondiba to run to their help even at midnight and Dhondiba never ever let anyone down.

At the same time, when Baba used to deal with the dabbawalas, he was extremely strict. We used to live in a ground-floor apartment, in 'Sneha Deep' building. There was a small shed behind the building where a lot of material belonging to the dabbawalas was stored. This shed was also used to conduct meetings of their association.

Whenever a dabbawala was caught doing anything wrong, if he had misbehaved after drinking too much, Baba used to get so angry that I used to tremble in fear. He did not use bad language and unlike the other dabbawalas never sweared. At the same time, he didn't mind twisting someone's ear or even giving a slap if that person had behaved badly. In fact, at times, he even gave the wrongdoer a kick on his back. All the dabbawalas were naturally scared of him when he was angry.

He was very rarely angry with me but even seeing him deal with others scared the life out of me. I was always careful about not getting on the wrong side of him. I got used to avoiding doing those things which Baba would not like.

Whenever I saw Baba's way of working, dealing with

people, I used to think, 'Even if I study further, I will never be able to achieve what he has done.' I used to think that I was so insignificant, so incapable. I had lost my confidence after failing in the matriculation exam.

I was attending Pinge's Classes regularly but I didn't see a very bright picture of my future. It was during this period that I saw Professor Dubhashi for the first time. He was not my teacher and I had only seen him in passing. He had a very impressive personality. Once, as my friend and I were walking, he passed us. I said to my friend, 'This teacher is as handsome as a hero, isn't he?'

My friend started laughing, 'That is exactly what he is, a hero!'

When I still looked puzzled, he explained further, 'Professor Satish Dubhashi is a very well-known actor on Marathi stage. Haven't you seen his play, "Tee Phulrani" (an adaptation of Shaw's Pygmalion)?'

Then and there, I decided to see that play. I asked Baba's permission and went to see 'Tee Phulrani'.

When the play began, I identified myself immediately with Manjula's, the heroine's character. I was so much like her, a village bumpkin, ignorant and clumsy! An oaf, who had still not mastered the polished city manners, the smart way of talking and who still dressed in the old-fashioned kurta-pyjama! I felt that the play was written with me in mind.

Even after I returned home, I couldn't get the play out of my mind. Manjula met the professor and he changed her life, would I meet a miracle-man like that? But then I thought some more and said to myself, 'Baba did not meet anyone like that and yet he managed to find the right path himself, didn't he?'

The truth finally dawned on me: if you have the will power and the strength to work towards your goals, you can achieve anything. All of a sudden, I felt calm. My mind was at peace. I had seen light. I decided to approach my studies, my work, with new enthusiasm. I began to understand the basics not only of the English language but the basics of the language of business as well.

6

To Deal or Not to Deal with Haji Mastan? That Was the Question!

It was during those days when I was struggling to master the English language at Pinge's Classes, that the phone rang in the Grant Road office of the Tiffin Box Suppliers' Association. My father picked up the receiver and heard a respectful voice at the other end, 'Salaam waleikum. This is Rashid miya speaking.'

Baba thought it was probably some customer, so he said, 'Yes, how can I help you?'

'Mastan Bhai has asked you and your colleagues to meet him.'

Baba was a little puzzled, 'Why? Does he want to send a dabba (tiffin box) somewhere?'

The voice at the other end hardened, 'Arrey, this is not about dabbas. Haji Mastan Bhai wants a meeting with the dabbawalas. Do you understand now?'

When he uttered the name Haji Mastan, he didn't need to clarify any further.

During those days, the smugglers were a force to reckon with and the uncrowned kings of Mumbai. Not only did they fight amongst themselves but at times even the common man suffered in their gang wars. That is why everyone trembled with fear at the very mention of their names.

Of course, my father was not one of those who trembled in fear at the mention of anybody's name. He knew some small-time smugglers because of his profession and was, in fact, good friends with Krishna Koli, the smuggler from Juhu Koliwada. But Baba was still puzzled as to why the kingpin of smugglers, Haji Mastan, would want to meet the dabbawalas.

A meeting of dabbawalas was convened and it was decided that three committee members would go to meet Haji Mastan. Haji Mastan welcomed the dabbawalas warmly. He enquired about their work and praised them and finally told them the purpose of the meeting, 'I would like to run your Tiffin Box Suppliers' Association in the name of my Trust. I will not interfere in any way in the day-to-day working of your association. I will help you in every possible way. Your members will be benefited by it. I would only like my name to be associated with your organisation.'

This was a totally unexpected proposal for the dabbawalas. Baba, Gangaram Talekar and the others exchanged startled glances. There was an awkward silence. But then Baba answered on behalf of the dabbawalas, 'We are sorry but we do not accept your proposal. Thank you for extending a helping hand but we cannot accept it.'

Having categorically refused Haji Mastan's proposal, the dabbawalas returned to their office and all hell broke loose. A marathon discussion followed. Everyone was curious to know, 'Why did Haji Mastan feel like helping out the dabbawalas?' There were many theories and conjectures:

Arrey, it must be a case of 'Sau chuhe khake, billi haj ko chali' (a cat after having eaten a hundred rats goes on a pilgrimage). He probably wants to go straight now!

I too feel the same. Haji Mastan Bhai wants to turn over a new leaf and become 'sharif' (respectable).

If he wants to become respectable, let him. But why should we get involved? We have a reputation to protect.

Our flawless reputation is exactly what he is after.

Yes, yes. I agree. He wants to kill two birds with one stone. Once his name is associated with us dabbawalas, he can claim to be doing honest hard work and at the same time, he can change all his black money into white!

See, it was good we refused his offer but what I am saying is that it would have helped us a lot financially.

Some agreed with this point of view.

Exactly. There were so many schemes we cannot implement because of the lack of funds. Now let's take the example of the dharamshalas we had planned to make all along the way from Alandi to Pandharpur. But till today, we have not been able to afford to build any dharamshala except for the one at Alandi.

You idiot, we are followers of the Saints Dnyaneshwar and Tukaram and sing their holy songs. We try to follow their teachings in our day-to-day life and now you want to join hands with the same people who go against those teachings?

Just then, there was a new thought. I think, Haji Mastan must have wanted to use our tiffin boxes for smuggling. See, we carry 70 to 80 thousand of these tiffin boxes from one end of the city to another. Who will be the wiser if we carry smuggled goods in 50 or 60 of these Dabbas?

Oh my God. I hadn't thought about that!

Just then, some one commented, 'You have seen too many Hindi films.' And everyone burst out laughing.

However, after giving the matter careful thought, the dabbawalas agreed that this was not really an impossible idea.

The debate raged on. There was a heated discussion of ideas, attacks and counter-attacks. But things did not go out of hand and finally everyone agreed that 'We were absolutely right to have refused Haji Mastan's helping hand.'

7

My College Days

I appeared twice for the English matriculation exam, in October and May, and finally passed. I could claim to be, at long last, 'matric passed'. The entire Medge clan was thrilled and extremely proud of my accomplishment. It was now my responsibility to see that I never let them down again and to fulfil their expectations.

I was admitted to the first year arts class in Parle College. Nandukaka Kulkarni dropped me to college on the first day in his Fiat. I got down from the car feeling like a prince. I was so excited, so eager to begin my college life. I entered the college and stopped still . . . I couldn't take another step forward.

The college was full of young girls and boys my age. All those smart, city-bred girls and boys were laughing, chatting, cracking jokes, entering the college with confidence and ease. Everyone was dressed so smartly in bright snazzy clothes, there was a riot of colours. In comparison to all those beautiful, colourful, butterflies, I felt like a beetle, in my old-fashioned shirt-pyjama.

I felt ashamed. Actually, no one had noticed me but I felt so conspicuous! I felt as if everyone was pointing in my direction and making fun of me. I hung my head down and went directly to my class. Most of the students knew one another. They were sitting in groups. I was the only one sitting all by myself, on a bench. I didn't know a soul and I looked so insignificant that nobody went out of their way to introduce themselves. I didn't look like the kind of person people wanted to get acquainted with.

I had gone to college with such high hopes and enthusiasm but I came back feeling crushed. Baba returned home late that night. I didn't go out to meet him. He called out to me, 'So Raghunathrao, how was your first day in college?'

I couldn't bring myself to speak. I just nodded. But then I got up the nerve and said, 'Baba, I want to get a pant stitched. Everyone in college wears pants. I was the only boy wearing a shirt and pyjama today.'

My father's eyes bored into mine. I thought he was going to pull my ears. But instead, he said, 'So what is wrong in that? It is the uniform of us dabbawalas. Why should you be ashamed of that?'

I was desperate. I didn't want to be the only one in college wearing old-fashioned pyjamas. I still remembered the early depressing days when I had gone from our tiny village of Aavadar to the school in the bigger town of Kadus. I didn't want history repeating itself.

But how was I to explain all this to my father? He had never gone to college. How would he understand the insecurities of a young boy? I made a last-ditch effort to convince him, 'Baba . . .'

But then he burst out laughing. He clapped me on the back, 'Silly boy! I was only joking. Go buy yourself new clothes tomorrow. OK?'

I started going to college on my bicycle, wearing my new pant-shirt. I now looked no different from the rest of the college students. However, apart from this superficial resemblance, I still had nothing in common with them.

The most important reason being my knowledge of the English language (or the lack of it!). Just because I had cleared the eleventh standard exam, it didn't mean that I was fluent in English. It was now six months since I had started attending college and I still couldn't for the life of me make head or tail of what the professors were saying in English. Then I found a solution to my problem: *Navneet Guides*. These guides contained all the questions and their detailed answers. By memorising these answers, I could score enough marks to pass in the exams.

In addition to this, I religiously took down the notes dictated by the professors in class. I then went to the library, referred to other books and struggled to make notes of my own. I came to be known as the studious 'nerd', who attended each and every class and always buried his head in study books.

I still had not made any friends and in fact not even many acquaintances. I still sat all alone on a bench.

Apart from studies, there were so many activities happening in college: dance, music, elocution, theatre, sports, etc. And of course, bunking classes and going for a film, chatting for hours over cups of chai in the canteen, these were favourite past-times of the students.

I knew only my classes and the library. I was going to college only to study. Just like Arjuna's (the Pandava warrior's) eye never left the archer's target, I never wavered from my aim of getting my BA degree with good grades.

Even though I was a college student, I was first and foremost a dabbawala and so I continued to work as one even while I was studying in college. I would pick up tiffin boxes from seven to ten in the morning and then attend classes in college till two o'clock in the afternoon. After a quick lunch, I was back at work; marking the tiffins, writing the codes, jotting down the finances. At five o'clock, I would gulp down a cup of tea and run to the typing classes. And directly to the college library after that! I would go over everything that had been covered in class on that day and only then go home and sleep.

I remained aloof from all the fun and frivolity of college life. But even amongst these serious study-filled days, there were a few romantic moments. My handwriting was good and I always took down all the notes in class, so very often, girls would ask me for my notebooks. If it had been a typical Mumbai boy, he would have used this to his advantage, but I couldn't stop myself from blushing whenever I handed my notebooks to the girls.

8

A New Beginning

For some unknown reason, I had chosen economics and geography, two totally unconnected subjects, for my BA. I was no longer a newcomer in college, nor in business. By this time I had got used to managing things in these two diametrically opposite worlds.

One morning, I reached Vile Parle railway station, dressed in our usual dabbawala's uniform of shirt, pyjama and Gandhi cap. We were sorting the tiffin boxes. 20-25 dabbawalas were getting ready to deliver some 500-600 tiffins to 50-60 different stations. Each dabbawala was packing the tiffins with his particular code into the crate. The work was going on like clockwork. I was supervising the whole operation.

Just then I saw Pendse, a student from my class, walking towards me. I automatically waved to him and smiled. He stopped, very puzzled. I saw that he had realised what my profession was and he couldn't hide his surprise.

I approached him and spoke without any trace of embarrassment, 'Hello. How come you are going so early to college today?'

'Amrute Sir is taking an extra class today. Have you forgotten about it?'

I did remember about it till this morning but in my work of sorting tiffins, I had completely forgotten about it. I thanked Pendse and asked him to go ahead. I would come to college on time for the lecture. He looked as if he didn't believe me and left.

I completed my work at the railway station in five minutes and sped home on my bicycle. In two minutes, I had changed from my dabbawala's uniform to my college student get-up. I rode the cycle like the wind and reached college in five minutes.

As I was entering class, I saw that Pendse had entered just before me. During the time it had taken him to walk to college from the railway station, I had successfully executed the entire transfer scene. I tapped him on the shoulder, he turned around and almost collapsed in amazement!

I couldn't help laughing. The other students were looking at us in surprise and they asked what the matter was. If I had been in the same situation two years earlier, I wouldn't have acknowledged Pendse at the station or if someone had seen me in my dabbawala uniform, I would not have been able to meet his eyes without feeling ashamed.

But now, I had managed to fit into both the roles of a student and a dabbawala. I was not ashamed any more of my profession. In fact, I was proud, and rightly so, of the fact that I worked, earned my living, studied in college and managed to pass in the exams. There was a new-found confidence in me.

I related the incident to the boys. Some of them were surprised but at the same time, they started laughing and I realised that they had accepted me for what I was.

While I was doing my final year BA, I got together all my courage and started asking the professors my difficulties. This was because some professors like Amrute Sir realised that my real problem was the English medium and didn't mind explaining to me in Marathi.

By now I had also learnt a lot about the dabbawalas' profession. In those days, around three thousand dabbawalas were shouldering the responsibility of delivering home-cooked food, on time, to approximately 80,000 or 90,000 office-goers in the vast city of Mumbai.

The admirable thing about it was, that this enormous task was undertaken by dabbawalas who were mostly illiterate. Very few of them had studied up to the fourth or fifth grade and many were 'angootha chaap', who couldn't even sign their names. Their Marathi dialect was coarse and their knowledge of English, non-existent. But in spite of this, a tiffin box which had been picked up from Hanuman Road, in Vile Parle, in the suburbs, reached Churchgate and from Churchgate, reached the exact person working on the third floor of the Sachivalay, the government office building, and exactly on time too.

The system that the dabbawalas had put into place was good enough, but I felt that I should put all my learning to good use and improve on the system to make it more efficient and error-free.

After giving the matter a lot of thought, I finally dared to raise the issue with my father, 'Baba, I think we should change our system of coding. We are using symbols right now. Someone uses a vertical line for his symbol, while others use triangles, arrows. Instead of this, we should gradually shift to a uniform code, which will be understood by all, making use of the English alphabets.'

I was scared of what Baba's reaction would be, if he would think that I was being too smart for my own good. Baba did not reply immediately, he thought for a while and then said, 'It is a good idea. But don't make any drastic changes and ask me before trying out anything new.'

I was relieved, 'I had been meaning to talk to you for so long but I hesitated. I was not sure that you would approve of any changes.'

Baba was frank, 'Son, our profession is now 80 to 85 years old. It could continue for so long only because we changed with the times. To begin with, the dabbawalas used to carry the dabbas on their head and walk the entire way, then we started using trams. Finally, it was the railways that fuelled the growth of our business. In the beginning, we used coloured threads to identify the dabbas, then we switched to symbols. Even these symbols have changed from time to time. Now you are much more educated than the rest of us. So, you must use your knowledge to improve the old system. But do it gradually, one at a time. Give the dabbawalas time to get used to one change and then move on.'

I agreed with him and started on this new project with enthusiasm.

9

The First Step Towards Modernisation

Mr Raghunath Medge had told me that the initiation of every dabbawala into their profession followed the same pattern; a hardy, enthusiastic youth from a small village in the Maval district came to Mumbai, stayed with some relative or the other and then started ferrying tiffin boxes as his rightful profession.

However, the very fact that they carry dabbas does not qualify them as dabbawalas, nor are they paid as much as the regular dabbawalas. These young men are assured of work when they come to Mumbai but it is then their responsibility to dedicate themselves to it and learn the rules and techniques of the profession.

Like in any other profession, the dabbawalas have to adhere to certain rules and regulations and follow the strict discipline, the rigid code of conduct. Every new dabbawala who joins the profession takes approximately six to eight months to imbibe these work ethics. During his stint as a trainee, he is paid a nominal stipend which just about covers his bare minimum cost of living. It is only when his training is complete that he gets the title of dabbawala and the regular salary of a dabbawala. The training is imparted by the veteran, experienced dabbawalas and the training certainly does not take place in any classroom. It is a totally hands-on learning experience, where the trainee picks up the tricks of the trade on the streets, in moving trains or on the stairs of the high-rise buildings of Mumbai.

The topics to be studies are varied ; How should one walk on the roads of Mumbai? How does one board the train? How does one assimilate the 'Bambaiyya' language? How does one win the confidence of customers of varied faiths, castes, creeds and religions?

Following in the footsteps of their ancestors, Shivaji's soldiers, who scaled tall cliffs and mountains to conquer forts, these young men from the region of Maval, today become proficient in climbing up the several flights of stairs of the high-rise buildings. A dabbawala becomes adept at boarding trains, carrying on his head, a huge crate, weighing 70-75 kgs, which contains 30-35 tiffin boxes. He walks for miles on end in the pouring Mumbai rain, drenched to the skin, and yet manages to deliver the lunch box to the customer.

The dabbawala is blessed with the courage and hardiness of his ancestors and at the same time he also possesses the humility and kindness preached by the great saints of Maharashtra. The profession of dabbawalas demands a reiteration and incorporation of these values.

Even if a dabbawala is illiterate, he has to be able to recognise the signs on the tiffin boxes, memorise the names of all the railway stations and be able to draw an exact map of Mumbai in his mind. He should know the railway timetable thoroughly and be able to calculate to the second, the time taken to load and unload the lunch boxes into the train. There is no way he can miss loading the boxes in a particular train at a particular time. In addition to all this, he should also be familiar with the market areas, the location of offices, etc.

Here is an interesting observation that one can reflect on; an illiterate person who relies entirely on his memory finds that it rarely lets him down; where as an educated person usually writes things down instead of storing them in his memory and then has difficulty finding the correct note when it is needed the most. An illiterate person automatically executes the task that he has been given at the correct time, in the correct manner because he has memorised all the details. One of the keys to the success of the dabbawalas could be the very fact that most of them are illiterate.

Instead of wasting their time in books, records, notes, they go ahead and complete the work assigned to them.

The dabbawalas' uniform is an integral part of their profession. A dabbawala in his typical uniform of pyjama, shirt and Gandhi cap stands out in the Mumbai crowds. For instance, at the busy Dadar railway station, a dabbawala wearing his traditional topi (cap) unerringly picks out another dabbawala because of his topi, from the thousands of people there; and rushes to his assistance. The two of them together, then make quick work of transferring the tiffins from one train to the other.

The dabbawalas' jargon is unique. A newcomer to the profession has to make a considerable effort to master it. If a tiffin box is made of aluminium, it is called a 'dabba' but if it is made of stainless steel, it is called a 'katka'. The long wooden crates that are loaded into the trains are called 'baakas' or 'khoka' and a customer is a 'baasan'. Even the buildings have different names in the dabbawala jargon. For example, Sunderabai School near Churchgate railway station is called 'Khambalyachi building' and the Apeejay House is known as 'Zendyache office' (the office of the flag).

A raw newcomer from the village imbibes all these techniques in six to eight months' time, becomes an official dabbawala and thus around thirty 'baasans' or customers are assured of receiving home-cooked food.

Once he had got the approval from his father, Raghunath Medge formulated and perfected his plan. He had decided to adhere to the basic framework of the dabbawalas' business which had proved so successful and gradually introduce some changes within this framework to enhance it. Thus the first change that he had in mind was to replace the age-old symbols which were used as identification marks by the dabbawalas with letters from the English alphabet.

In the year 1977-78, the dabbawalas were divided into groups based on the mukadam system. Every mukadam employed 25 to 30 dabbawalas and paid their salaries. Let us take the example of Vile Parle (East): Here the two main mukadams operating were Medge and Nimbalkar. The tiffin boxes transported by the Medge dabbawalas were marked with green symbols while the Nimbalkar tiffin boxes were marked with white symbols. It was simple enough till this point. However, the symbols that followed were randomly strung together. Let us take this example:

Green colour- Medge's group

Pa	Parle
1	The number of the dabbawala in the group who was responsible for picking up the tiffin box
•	Hanuman Road
Δ	Churchgate
3	Dabbawala number three in the Churchgate group
*	Sachivalay
4	4th floor

We will now see how this tiffin box, marked with green symbols reached from Hanuman Road in Vile Parle to the correct office in Sachivalay.

Dabbawala number one from Medge's Vile Parle group collected the tiffin from Mr Joshi's home and along with 25 to 30 other tiffin boxes took it to the railway station. Here the other 20 dabbawalas from the Medge group assembled with the 30 dabbas each that they had collected. Similarly, the 30 dabbawalas from the Nimbalkar group were also there with the 30 dabbas each that they had picked up. Now these approximately 1,200 dabbas were sorted. Dabbawala number one from the Medge group picked up the 25 to 30 tiffin boxes for Churchgate, put them in his crate and got into the train bound for Churchgate. The other dabbawalas too followed the same pattern and got into their designated train, carrying the dabbas they were in charge of.

Dabbawala number one got down at Churchgate with his crate. At Churchgate station, there were thousands of tiffin boxes which come from all parts of the city. Now, dabbawala number one picked up the tiffins for the area assigned to him and left on his cycle, while dabbawala number three, who was in charge of the Sachivalay area picked up his lot of 25 to 30 tiffin boxes and headed towards Sachivalay. He went to the fourth floor and handed over Mr Joshi's lunch box to him. The lunch box that had been picked up from the customer's home at around nine o'clock in the morning reached his office at lunchtime, after having travelled by bicycle, train, a bicycle once again or a handcart, and carried by two or three different dabbawalas through this long journey.

This system which dated to the time of Dhondiba Medge was good enough, but Raghunath strove to make it more efficient and free from errors.

Each group decided its own symbols under the prevalent system. Thus while one group used a white spot to indicate where the lunch box was picked up from, another group used 2 parallel lines.

Raghunath suggested that common symbols be used which would be understood by all, and that English letters be used instead of Marathi letters. Areas were assigned different letters. For example, in Vile Parle, the Gujarati Society area was given the code A while, Dixit Road next to it was given the code B, Malaviya Road the code C and so on and so forth. This area-based categorisation was easy to understand and to memorise. The difficult part was getting the dabbawalas to accept it. The dabbawalas, most of whom, had not studied beyond the second or third standard were mortally scared of the English letters. In order to get rid of this phobia, Raghunath began coaching the dabbawalas. He was busy enough with college and the dabbawala business. Now to add to it all, he also had to teach the illiterate dabbawalas English.

However, where there is a will, there is a way. Raghunath put in 25 hours of work in a 24-hour day and achieved the impossible.

This change was met with a barrage of doubts and negative comments.

- We don't understand nothing
- What if the train leaves by the time we manage to decode these letters? My 'baasan' (customer) will starve!

But Raghunath was firm in his resolve. He was sure that his plan would be successful.

Gradually, even the dabbawalas were convinced of the advantages of this change in their system.

After a long campaign, Raghunath succeeded in winning over the confidence of the dabbawalas from Vile Parle. He said to them, 'Just as a child passes from the first to the second and then to the third grade until he graduates, we too will take it one step at a time. Once you have learnt and assimilated one thing, we will go on to the next. If we progress like this, just see how we will grow. We will all benefit from it.'

Raghunath had taken the first step towards the

modernisation of their business and had managed to climb the first step in the ladder, taking along with him, at least one group of dabbawalas.

Dhondiba Medge patted Raghunath on the back and praised his efforts, 'Well done. This is the way we will go ahead, one station at a time.'

10

My Childhood Days

After a long time, I got a letter from my mother. I opened it in haste, read it and was extremely disturbed. I lay down on my bed and pretended to sleep so that no one would see that I was upset.

As if I could sleep! I tossed and turned. Once Baba entered the room and was surprised to see me sleeping, 'What is the matter with Raghu? How come he went to sleep so early?' But, thankfully, he didn't try to wake me and left the room after putting off the light.

I tried to go to sleep but one sentence from Aai's letter echoed in my mind, 'I miss you with all my heart, my son.'

She had got the letter written from someone. But I could still recognise her words, her emotions and see her tired, sad face in it. I felt very guilty.

I buried my face in the pillow but the images of all those moments spent with her in Kadus and Avadar flashed before my eyes.

Our original village was Avadar. It is a very small village. We used to live there in a joint family, with our cousins and their families, 20 to 25 members in all. My father and uncle were working as dabbawalas in Mumbai.

The villagers would grow rice and millet but everything depended on the rains. Baba would scrimp and scrounge in Mumbai and send a money order to us which would take care of the huge family in the village.

Avadar lacked even the basic amenities. There was no electricity, no running water, no roads. If someone fell ill, one had to walk 20-25 miles to the nearest town and fetch a doctor. The doctor would come on horseback. If the matter was really serious, four men had to carry the patient on a make-shift stretcher and take him to the clinic, which was 25 miles away.

I remember, during one monsoon, I had a tapeworm in my foot. What a terrible time I had! It took two weeks for it to get better and all that time I was in agony! Thankfully the school was closed for the rainy season. Actually, we had more holidays than working days in that tiny school in Avadar. All classes from first to the fourth took place in one single room and there was only one teacher!

In those days, I was not very close to my father. Baba seemed like a guest who would visit us from time to time. But since this guest always got us gifts, clothes and sweets, I waited for him eagerly. I used to love to touch his spotless, sparkling white clothes. The stiffly-starched clothes tickled my hand. All the other men in my village used to wear faded, dirt-streaked, sweat-stained clothes. My father was the only man in the village who wore such spotlessly clean clothes. My father stood out in the village not only because of his clothes but also because of his physical appearance and his behaviour. He was tall and fair. Some villagers would say that he was as fair as a 'Sahib'. I had no idea who this 'Sahib' was, but my father seemed like a king to me.

I used to dream about Baba. I would visualise him in the city, living in a huge palace, with scores of servants waiting on him, a golden chariot with four pure white horses outside the door. If somebody had told me then that your father lives with your uncle in a tiny tin-roofed room in Mumbai, I would not have believed him and in fact would have been very angry with him.

I was dazzled by my father, not just by his looks but also by his personality. In those days, he had donated a princely sum of Rs 500 at one go to extend the small one-room school in the village temple. He had also arranged an entertainment show, inviting artistes from Mumbai and sold tickets in 40 villages in order to raise funds for the school. He seemed to tower above all the other villagers then.

When I passed with good marks from our village school, everyone praised me, 'The kid is smart. He will go far if he is sent to a good school in a big town.'

My parents too felt the same so my mother and I went to Kadus. Kadus was a much bigger place than Avadar, almost like a city. There was a good school here. It was the town of the Vidhan Sabha member, Mr Rambhau Mhalgi. The majority of the population belonged to the Brahmin caste. Most of the people were well-educated and cultured.

We had no place to stay in Kadus. I stayed with my mother in somebody's out-house. Aai enquired in the school and one day took me along and made me sit in the second standard there.

I was awe-struck! What an enormous school! The classroom was airy, spacious. There were benches for the students to sit on and desks to keep their books on.

The master entered the classroom. All the students stood up to wish him. He asked everyone to sit down, then turned to me and asked, 'What is your name?'

I stood up and said, 'Raghunath Dhondiba Medge.'

'Where are you from?'

As I was replying to the teacher's question, I heard a suppressed giggle. And then the whole class burst out laughing.

I didn't understand why they were laughing at me. I sneaked a look at my clothes. Aai had dressed me in brand-new clothes because it was my first day in a big school. I was wearing a striped cotton pyjama, a dark blue shirt, a silver anklet, a silver bracelet and a gold chain. What could be the matter? I was as smart as can be!

As the laughter showed no signs of dying down, the master shouted, 'Quiet everybody!' The children sobered down but I saw the glimpse of a smile even on the teacher's face.

For the first six months, I wore the same costume to school. Like my clothes, my language too was coarse.

Whenever the students heard me say words like 'mapla, tupla, mahe . . .' They would tease me and call me 'Mavlya'.

Finally, after six months, Aai got a school uniform stitched for me. I looked at myself in the mirror, white shirt, khaki shorts. For the first time, I looked like a school student.

We were much better off now. We had rented an old house for Rs 5 per month. Baba had bought 10 acres of land at Kadus and paid Rs 9,000 for it. A few cousins came from the village to study in Kadus. There were also a few farm-hands who had come down from the village to help with the farming. Our house in Kadus was filled with people. Aai ably supervised the children's education and the farming as well.

Initially I used to feel a little awkward. I had to bear with the ragging in class. But I was never scared and never missed school for fear of ragging. Slowly I got used to the new school life. I became friends with the students and started going to their houses. I now felt as if I belonged to this town.

Our house was located in Brahmin Ali, the Brahmin dominated area of the town. Our neighbours were Brahmins with surnames like Kulkarni, Godse, Joshi, etc. As I started visiting my Brahmin friends' houses, I unconsciously picked up some facets of their way of life. The Brahmins were known for the purity of their language, the neatness and cleanliness of their houses, the hypnotic chanting of poems and shlokas, the inspiring debates and discussions on various socio-political issues. I was very impressed by all these things.

Sometimes I would compare the atmosphere in our house to the atmosphere in the Brahmin houses. Even though we had moved from a small village to a big town like Kadus, our house was still essentially like a rustic farmer's house, full of confusion and disorder.

Aai used to wake up early in the morning to make a huge pile of bhakris for everyone in the house. After we kids left for school, she would then leave for the fields. Sometimes, she would get very late, supervising the workers, getting things done in the fields. Then I would draw water from the well and store it. I would cut the vegetables and get almost half of the meal ready. If my father was in town, he would say, 'Don't you want a new cycle? So go to the field and do the night-watch. Everyone should work hard and earn their leisure by working hard first.' So I would go to the fields at night and work by moonlight with the farmhands, cleaning the grains, sorting them.

During the Ganesh festival every house on our road celebrated by bringing home a Ganapati idol, every house that is, except ours. There were pujas, maha-aartis, prasad in all my friends' houses. I used to love it. Once, my father had come home during this time. Preparations were going on in full swing in each household. I decided that this year I too would get an idol of Ganapati. But I didn't have the money and felt too scared to ask my father. So I sneaked my hand into the pocket of my father's kurta which was hanging behind the door and took out a coin. It was a four-anna coin. I quickly hid it in my father's Venkatesh Stotra book.

The next day, my father began reading the Venkatesh Stotra and naturally found the hidden coin. He called me and in a stern voice asked me how it had got there. I denied knowing anything about the matter but he guessed the truth. He was very angry and for the first and last time in my life, I got a hiding from my father. Feeling humiliated, I crept into a corner and started sobbing. When my mother came in, she asked my father why he had hit me. My father began telling her the story but towards the end, he couldn't help laughing,

'What an idiot that boy is! Stealing money from my pocket and then hiding it again in my book, where I am sure to find it!'

My mother too started laughing. I looked at the two of them. I couldn't understand it. This was too much. I had got the beating and they found the whole thing amusing!

11

My Father's Wedding

The ten years spent as a student in Kadus are full of bitter-sweet memories. I began to like the school, the studies and enjoy the company of my friends.

But I could not, for the life of me, understand the financial situation in our household. Since we were farmers, there was always plenty on the table but when it came to hard cash, we were always short of it. If my uniform tore, it was patched up and I had to wear that patched uniform for months. We used to have a lot of visitors and I used to welcome them because they very often gave me some money when they left. Someone gave me five paise, others ten. I would shake my head and say 'no' when they offered me the money but when they insisted, I would accept it gladly and cram it in my pocket and keep it safely with the rest of my treasure.

I used to do a lot of work at home, from cleaning to cooking. And my most important job was to keep the accounts. From the time I was in fourth standard, my father had entrusted me with this duty of noting down the family and farm accounts. This was because, even at that time, I was the most educated one in the family!

In the beginning I was scared to take on this responsibility but my father insisted, 'What do you go to school for? Come on, take that ledger and start entering the debit and credit details.'

I used to faithfully enter the details of all the transactions every day; the wages paid to the labourers, cost of the new tiles for the house, money owed to someone, etc. My father used to double-check the accounts occasionally and nod with satisfaction. This confidence that he had in me was the greatest gift I could have got. At such times, my mother would look at me with such love and admiration in her eyes!

The entire credit for my education up to the BA level goes to my mother. Even though I was her only son and the apple of her eye, when it came to school and studies, she was very strict. It is only because of her that I continued my studies, reluctantly at first and then with genuine interest.

Many of my cousins never adjusted to life in Kadus. They would always find excuses to miss school. Very often, they returned to Avadar. At that time, I used to think that they were really lucky but with Aai, I didn't stand a similar chance!

Finally, only Aai and I remained in the house in Kadus. That may be the reason for the close bond between us. We used to tell each other everything; all the incidents at school, in the fields, gossip about relatives. We only had one another to share everything with.

When I was in the eighth standard, Aai was very upset about something. She didn't confide in me as usual. She used to be lost in thought and she used to look sad and depressed.

I tried to ask her but she would say nothing. Baba too, had not visited us in a long time.

One day, when I returned from school, she was packing clothes in her bag, her best sari, my shirts, trousers ... I stood still in surprise. She looked up, 'Raghu, we are going to the village tomorrow. Will these clothes be enough?'

I didn't understand what was going on, 'Tomorrow? To the village? To Avadar?'

She snapped at me, 'Don't ask too many questions. Just do as I say.'

My face crumpled and as I turned to go, she caught my hand. She pulled me close, ruffled my hair and started speaking, 'Your father is getting married again. We must go for the wedding. Your cousins are very angry and your grandmother refuses to talk to anyone. But when he decides something, can anything make him change his mind?'

I was shocked, 'My father getting married again!' I couldn't believe it!

My mother was still talking but she seemed to be talking more to herself than to me. It was as if a dam had burst. She had kept her emotions locked up for so long! I didn't understand everything that she was saying but the gist of the matter was that Baba was unhappy because they couldn't have another child after me. He was worried about how the family line would continue if something happened to me. Tragedies like this often struck families in the villages. So he had decided to marry again. He had seen a young girl, half his age and had finalised the marriage.

I will never forget my father's wedding which took place in a dharamshala in the town of Alandi. I remember my mother dressed in a brand new sari, the crestfallen look on her face, tears flowing down her cheeks.

My father had bought me new clothes from Mumbai for his wedding. After I wore them, I did a little jig and started feeling a little better. When my father and his new bride garlanded each other, I threw the coloured rice in their direction, with enthusiasm.

My mother and I were the only two guests from my father's side for the wedding and there were two or three guests from the bride's side. My father introduced me to my stepmother, 'Raghu, this is your younger Aai. You can call her Bai.' I nodded my head.

The strange thing was, or it may have been the custom in those days, but the fact is that my new 'mother' came with my mother and me to Kadus while my father went back to Mumbai.

Once back in Kadus, there were constant flare-ups between my mother Kondabai and my stepmother Suman. Baba was away in Mumbai but I was caught in the crossfire.

Aai was the most precious person in the world to me and I hurt so badly whenever she suffered. But at the same time, I couldn't hurt my stepmother either. Firstly, she was my father's wife after all and then she was always so loving and kind to me.

Sometimes there would be a massive fight and then my

mother would take me by the hand and leave for her parents' house. I would miss school and spend the rest of the days worrying about my studies and exams.

I used to be very tense whenever I thought of all the studies that I was missing because I wanted to score good marks and do well in the exams. Finally I decided that I would not let the adults' quarrels affect my studies and most important of all I would not interfere in their quarrels and try to get along with everyone.

This attitude helped me deal not only with the situation at that time but proved extremely useful in every difficult moment in the future.

Later, my father called my stepmother to live with him in Mumbai. I too used to spend my holidays there. Bai, my stepmother, had a baby daughter, Shakuntala, who was as dear to me as if she was my own sister. Whenever I was in Mumbai, I happily took charge of dropping her to school and picking her up after school. While I was studying in college in Mumbai, my mother would also visit us sometimes and at times I would go and spend my vacations in Kadus.

If I couldn't visit her in a long time, my mother would get someone to write me a letter on her behalf. Her letter was never complete without this one sentence, 'I miss you with all my heart, my son.'

Now, after tossing and turning and trying to sleep, I finally decided not to wait till morning and write to her immediately. 'Dear Aai, I miss you a lot too. Don't worry. I will try and come to Kadus next week.' When I saw what I had written, I winced. I knew very well that however good my intentions, next week, something or the other would come up and I wouldn't be able to keep my word.

My mother, though, would wait for me with impatience. Because for her, I was the only person in her life, she could consider her very own.

12

The Dream That Never Came True

The day I passed the BA examination was the happiest day of my life. I had passed with first class honours!

I came home and took my father's blessings. I touched the feet of my mother, who had come down from Kadus, and my stepmother and then left immediately to take admission to the law college for the LLB course.

Now, my routine changed a little. My day began by attending classes in the Jeetendra Chauhan Law College, in Vile Parle (W), then I went on to updating the dabbawalas' account books, calculating the salaries of the employees, going to the typing and shorthand classes . . .

This hectic routine was not new to me. I had been doing it for the past four years. But, now, I seemed to be fired with a new enthusiasm.

I was the first to fail the matriculation exam, the first to pass the matric exam and now I was also the first to graduate in my family.

Even in the midst of my whirlwind schedule, I still found time to daydream . . . I imagined . . . 'I have finished my law studies, I have started my own practice, there is a never-ending line of clients in my brand new office. Initially I would take up all sorts of cases but later I would specialise; fight civil cases or become an advocate specialising in criminal cases. I have built an enviable reputation for myself. I am pleading the case on behalf of my client in impeccable English, my opponent cannot find a way to counter my brilliant arguments, the judge reads out his ruling and I win the case for my client . . .'

Suddenly, there is a loud knock at the door. I am roused with a shock from my pleasant daydream. A man with a heavy moustache rasps in his hoarse voice, 'I want to send a dabba. Here is the address.'

The future 'advocate' had no choice but to meekly note down the address.

My father was very pleased that I had finished my college education. He decided to get me married. I tried to make him change his mind, 'Let me finish my law course. I am still not earning enough, etc.'

But he silenced me with an argument more clever than any lawyer's, 'A man's education is never complete in life. Why only LLB? Study even further! You have all my blessings. Getting married doesn't mean you have to stop studying. Your second point was your income. Well, you are earning enough to support your wife even now. Isn't it?'

I had no option but to say 'yes'. That was the signal my father was waiting for. He went ahead and was, in fact, so full of enthusiasm that he planned not one, not two but three weddings! My two cousins' and mine! We immediately started getting proposals.

I went to Manchar to 'see' a girl, Sharada, whose family was known to us. I liked her and the mahurat of the wedding was decided. Actually, the mahurats of three weddings were decided. My cousins would get married in Manchar on the same day, at the same venue on 22 April. But since there is a saying, 'Teen tigada, Kaam bigada' (doing anything in threes is inauspicious) my wedding date was set for 11 June.

My father's enthusiasm knew no bounds. As the head of the Medge clan, he was responsible for looking after the wedding preparations. He was generous in his spending, providing for the shopping, jewellery, the mandaps, the catering, etc.

I couldn't help being distracted and it definitely affected my studies.

11 June 1979! I got married in a temple in Alandi, before Sant Dnyaneshwar's Samadhi. There were around 2,500 guests for our wedding. They had come from Mumbai and Pune especially for the occasion, our relatives, friends, neighbours, people from our village and 1,000 dabbawalas!

My father had arranged taxis for the guests who had come from distant places. Everyone reached by nine o'clock in the morning, had breakfast and then attended the wedding. There was lunch to follow. This was at the Dabbawala Association's Dharamshala. My father-in-law was a textile trader. In keeping with his prestige and that of my father, he had arranged a grand lunch with five different varieties of desserts. Normally, during our weddings, lunch consists of dal, rice and sweet boondi, that is all. The menu at my wedding with a spread of sweets like laddoos, Mysore pak, karanji, jalebis, etc., pleased the guests and everyone ate to their heart's content.

Because of the venue, at Sant Dnyaneshwar's Samadhi, the huge guest list of 2,500 and the grand lunch, my wedding was talked about for months after that.

During the wedding lunch, all the women were asked to recite 'ukkhanas', short verses which had the name of their husband in it because normally the women would not call their husband by his name. This session was filled with light-hearted humour and wit. My wife recited a witty 'ukkhana' with my name in it and then everyone started pestering me to recite a couplet with my wife's name in it. But I got away with only calling out her name, 'Sharada'.

Finally, by evening, all the guests had left and we went to Kadus. After staying there for 15 days, we Mumbaikars came back to Mumbai. My married life began in our small one-bedroom flat in Vile Parle, which we shared with my father, stepmother, stepsister Shakuntala and three cousins from the village who were studying in Mumbai!

There are so many golden memories of those days. After marriage, your life changes drastically, you share everything with this new entrant in your life. It is very important to get to know her, understand her and form a bond with her, which will last forever. We used to find the time from my work and her housework and go out, to the cinema or somewhere else.

My father decided that I could now shoulder the responsibility of the household in Mumbai and he started spending most of his time in the village. He looked after the farming and did a lot of social work and involved himself in the social and political issues of the village. He was still the president of the Dabbawalas' Associaton and whenever he was needed in Mumbai, he would come down and attend meetings or complete the work and then return to the village.

I was now in charge of all the dabbas that my father handled in Vile Parle, all the employees, their salaries. I was responsible for solving their disputes and handling all the other problems. I was now playing the dual role of head of the business and at home too. I was no longer an assistant to my father. I suddenly realised that I would have to behave as befits a head of the family. But easier said than done! I used to wait eagerly for Baba to come to Mumbai and whenever he was in town, I felt more relaxed.

My wife was familiar with Mumbai since her sister lived in Worli and she used to visit her before our marriage. What she was unfamiliar with, was the way the home was run in Mumbai. She was a willing student, prepared to learn. But she still made small mistakes, spilling something, forgetting to put salt in a particular dish. At such times, my stepmother would get irritated. Sharada never argued with her but tears would stream down her face. Sometimes, I would hear of the small tiffs or at times I could guess it from the strained atmosphere at home. But I did not interfere. I could see things from my wife's point of view, she was new to the family and didn't have anyone except me to confide in and understand her problems. I could not bring myself to pull her up over trivial issues. At the same time, I could understand my stepmother's impatience. How would Sharada learn unless her mistakes were pointed out to her? I could not say anything to my stepmother, that would amount to disrespect and it would hurt her.

So I would try and find the golden mean. I would listen to both of them and not comment in anybody's favour. Instead I would cajole, explain and settle the matter amicably.

This philosophy of finding the golden mean, settling issues amicably proved extremely beneficial to me later, when I had to deal with thousands of dabbawalas and ensure that they all stay together like one big family.

Three months after my wedding I learned that I was to become a father. Everyone in the family was overjoyed.

My father had longed for many children. 'What if something happens to Raghu!' It was this thought that had compelled him to remarry. Ironically, my stepmother too had only one daughter, Shakuntala. So, my father's dream of a house filled with the laughter of several children, had remained a dream. Now Baba, Aai and my stepmother eagerly awaited the arrival of their first grandchild.

It was the end of September. The rains had stopped. Sharada and I were returning one evening from the cinema, where we had gone to see *Suhag*, a new film of Amitabh Bachchan. I told her, 'I am thinking of giving another exam along with LLB. It is called the CA entrance exam. I have filled up the form and even started studying for it.'

Sharada asked, 'What is this CA?'

I said, 'As if I know. My friend, Yogesh Shah told me to appear for this exam. He said that if I pass, I should study for the CA exams. He was saying that you get a very good job if you pass the CA exam.'

Sharada's face lit up with happiness, 'You are already BA. Then you will be LLB and then CA? My God! That is so educated, isn't it? You will be the most educated member not only among our two families but among most of the families in our entire taluka (district)! Tell me, will you get an "afsar's" (officer's) job in an office?'

To tell the truth I was not entirely sure. But one should always dream big, so I echoed her thoughts, 'Why only an "afsar"? I could even get a manager's post. An air-conditionned office, my very own cabin, two telephones on the desk, a revolving chair! A flat on Worli sea-face and an Ambassador car!' It was such a beautiful vision, that for a second I almost believed it was true. I looked at Sharada and saw the same dream reflected in her eyes. She had such a contented look! I loved her and at that moment, I felt sorry for her too. She had studied only till the ninth standard and then she had got married. After marriage, she hadn't studied further. She was named Sharada, after the Goddess of learning, but she had not been lucky enough to get even an SSC certificate!

But in spite of that, she was so proud of her educated husband! She felt glory in my success. She was happy believing in my dream. I decided to myself that from the next day, I would begin studying in earnest and work towards achieving this dream of ours.

It is said that the dreams one has at the first light of dawn often come true. I didn't realise it then, but we had not seen this dream of ours at that auspicious moment!

13

An Irreparable Loss

After my marriage, my father preferred to stay longer in the village and his visits to Mumbai for the Dabbawalas' Association's work, were few and far between.

During the 40 years that he was in Vile Parle, his favourite haunt was a sugarcane juice stall opposite the railway station. He was invariably to be found there. New clients approached him there, if any existing client had a complaint he would go there, and many of the quarrels amongst dabbawalas were solved there.

As Baba started spending more time in the village, this place became deserted. However, his reputation and prestige was growing rapidly in the village, and no one was more admired and respected in the village, in fact in the entire region, than my father. He had tried his hand at politics earlier, but with little success. Now, he played an important role in the social and political scene of the region.

While Baba was in the village, the policemen could take things easy because if there were any disputes, fights, quarrels, Baba would intervene and solve the problem. He was of the opinion that matters should not go as far as becoming a police case in his village. It almost became a prestige issue with him.

He adopted different strategies to deal with different problems. He didn't mind resorting to a slap in the face or even a kick if the situation demanded it. The offender too used to listen to him because it was preferable to being in the police lock-up.

I remember an incident that took place during the Dassehra festival in the year 1979. There was a bullock-cart race in the village. These races were always fiercely contested and there was invariably a fight at the end of the day.

So this year, a friend of mine from school, Mohan Gargote had taken part in the race. Mohan was a farmer and he used to come to Mumbai sometimes to look after some trade union work. A villager who comes back from the glamorous city of Mumbai usually brags, shows off and makes sure that some of the city's glamour rubs off on him. Mohan was no exception.

The bullock-cart race began. Mohan was confident of winning. But his confidence was short-lived. The Koli folk, the fishermen of the village won the race. Naturally a fight ensued. Mohan found an excuse to quarrel, the Kolis flexed their muscles; swears, curses were exchanged until both sides were ready to battle it out.

When Baba heard of the fight, he ran to the scene. Mohan

was heartened by his arrival and he rushed aggressively towards the Kolis. Baba caught him by the collar and gave him two resounding slaps. 'Raghu's father hit me instead of dealing with those Koli men?' Mohan was shamefaced. Baba thundered, 'Eh you, don't try and show off your Mumbai "masti" (airs) here.' As Mohan opened his mouth to speak, Baba yelled, 'Chup! Shut up! Don't you dare say another word!'

Not just Mohan, but everyone else too fell silent. Some who had been all geared up for a fight looked dazed. Baba addressed the Koli men in a humble tone, 'It is entirely his mistake and he has been punished for it. Please forget it and go home now.'

When the crowd had disappeared, Baba spoke to Mohan, 'Arey, Mohanya, my son. You must be asking yourself, "Why did Raghu's father who is like my own father, take not my side, but theirs? Why did he hit me and not them?"'

Mohan must have been asking himself exactly the same question so he nodded his head without saying a word.

Baba laughed, 'You idiot, the mistake was yours and if I had not interfered those tough Koli men would have beaten you black and blue. So I said to myself that it is better that he gets a slap from this old uncle of his rather than a vicious beating from the Kolis.'

Mohan was still puzzled and didn't understand this logic so Baba explained, 'Look here, I scolded you, slapped you. So the Koli men's anger was appeased. They went away quietly. Those two slaps of mine saved the day today. Just think, the fight was averted, there was no police case, no injuries, nothing. The matter was solved without all these headaches!'

Mohan gazed at my father in admiration. He didn't feel angry or humiliated any more, all he felt was respect and gratitude for my father's wisdom.

Till date, Mohan proudly tells everyone, 'I will never in my life forget that slap in the face I got from Raghu's father.'

Once when Baba came to Mumbai, I thought that he was looking very pale and weak so I took him to a doctor. The doctor examined him and then asked us to get his blood and urine checked. When the reports came in, he was diagnosed with jaundice. The doctor, being a friend, advised my father, 'Dhondiba, the only remedy for jaundice is rest and a strict control over the diet. Stay put here in Mumbai for a while.'

Baba nodded his head. He took an enforced rest of barely eight days and then declared himself fit and left for the village. A friend of his was contesting the elections in the village and Baba had taken on the responsibility of campaigning for him. An election campaign is always hectic. One has to tour many villages, eat whatever is available, drink water at all kinds of places . . .

In January, Baba had come to Mumbai. His trip was hectic to say the least. He went from one railway station to another, met up with hundreds of dabbawalas, attended the monthly meeting of the Dabbawalas' Association and settled quite a few disputes.

It was 9 January. Baba vomited blood. We were all terrified and we immediately got him admitted into Nanavati Hospital.

11 January, in the evening, Baba complained of uneasiness

so I got the doctor to come and see him. When the doctor started to examine him, Baba relaxed. He closed his eyes and seemed to be sleeping, when the doctor quietly said, 'He is no more.'

It took 40 seconds for the meaning of those 4 words to sink in. And then there was pandemonium. My father, with his larger-than-life image, had fallen ill and passed away, all in a matter of two days.

Of course, we realised later that it was not just a matter of two days! The sickness had been eating him up from the inside for months. Baba had ignored his ailment and gone ahead with his work of helping others.

We could not believe it! The shock was too much to bear for our family. Baba who had been his usual self till a couple of days back was no longer among us. The news of Baba's death spread like wildfire throughout the city of Mumbai and in dozens of villages in Maval. Everyone was overcome with grief!

It was only fitting that his last rites be done in his beloved village. So after completing all the formalities, we took the dead body in an ambulance to Kadus.

It saddened me when we started referring to my father as the 'dead body'. Not just the hospital staff, but even when the near and dear ones started saying 'dead body', I was overcome with grief. Of course, nobody did it deliberately or with any intention of hurting me. It is just the way things are. But to me, it was cruel that my father, who had been a unique, awe-inspiring person, was nothing more to the world than a 'dead body' the moment he stopped breathing.

Well, we reached Kadus at around 3.30 or 4.00 a.m. on the morning. It was still dark. But the first thing we saw by the light of the streetlight was the sight of thousands of people waiting silently. As soon as they heard the news, thousands of people had left from Mumbai, Pune and the neighbouring villages, taken whatever means of transport was available, reached Kadus and waited patiently to see him for the last time. I could not hold back my tears.

Thousands of mourners were part of his funeral procession. Everyone wanted to pay their last respects to this great man.

Two days later, somebody called from Mumbai and said that the news of my father's demise had been printed prominently in many of the city's newspapers. The dabbawalas had not worked for one day. What was very touching was that the traders in Vile Parle had paid their last respects to Baba by closing down the entire market for a day.

My father, Dhondiba Medge's true riches could be counted not in money but rather in the good wishes, respect and blessings of thousands of people!

14

Head of the Family—A Difficult Role

On the 10th and 13th day after my father's demise, we gave the traditional lunch to everyone who came to pay their condolences, which amounted to around four thousand people! All the rites were over now and the lunch symbolised the return to the normal routine of life. All the guests had left. I was thinking that I too would return to Mumbai in a couple of days.

The next morning, Kankiya Seth, the owner of the grocery shop in the village came to see me, 'So, how are things, Raghunath Seth?'

I was embarrassed, 'Please don't call me "seth". Since when did I become one?'

'Since your father is no more, you are now the owner, the "seth".'

After some general conversation, Kankiya Seth got up to go. At the door, he hesitated and then in a casual tone, 'Of course, there is no hurry . . . But whenever it is possible . . .'

I was bewildered, 'What is the matter? Please speak frankly!'

'Relax! There is no cause to worry . . .'

As a matter of fact, I had not been tense until that moment but now I was apprehensive. Kankiya Seth pushed a piece of paper in my hand, said, 'There is no hurry!' and left.

When I looked at the figure on the piece of paper, I was stunned. It was the outstanding amount we owed him for the groceries which ran into a few thousands!

I showed it to my mother. She said, 'Raghu, at the time of the three weddings in the family, we had taken things on credit and since then, the figure has increased and now with this lunch, it must have gone up even further!'

Over the next few days, other shop-owners came by saying, 'We were in the neighbourhood, we were just passing by, thought we would drop in to say hello . . .' The 'mandap' decorators in the village, the clothes shop-owner and a few others.

All these men were well known to the family. They used to enter with a tense face but when they left, it was my forehead which would be creased with worry. We owed all of them a lot of money. After my father's death, it was now my responsibility to repay them. Thankfully, we were on good terms with all of them. They all had trusted my father. They had come to me and told me the facts only because they had no alternative.

Everyone said, 'There is no hurry. But . . .' I understood. There was no use denying the facts. I promised them, 'I will pay back your money as soon as possible.'

I returned to Mumbai. Here too, among the many who came to pay their condolences, there were some who pressed a piece of paper into my hand while leaving . . . they didn't need to say anything else! A jeweller, a tailor . . .

Baba is no more . . . Just four small words but what a devastating change they had caused in my life. I was very tense, I couldn't sleep at night. I couldn't see any solution to the problem. I didn't know what to do, who to talk to . . .

I went to see Nandu Kaka Kulkarni. He was in his shop, 'Eastern Radio', surrounded by several radios, televisions, tape-recorders which had to be repaired. As soon as he saw me, he put aside his work, asked me to sit down and sent for a cup of tea.

I told him about my problems and my father's debts that I had to repay. He didn't seem surprised, 'Look Raghu, your father was a king-hearted man. He was generous to a fault. He shouldered the responsibility of the three weddings and didn't think of money when it came to spending for the family.'

I agreed, 'Yes Kaka. You are right. It is our custom to have a grand wedding and other ceremonies and spend lavishly on them, even if we have to take a loan for it. How could my father be an exception?'

'Raghu, I would like to tell you two more things, your father was capable of paying back that money and he had every intention of doing so. He didn't dream that he would no longer be around to do that and that the burden would come on to you. The second thing you should know is that he too had helped many people financially. There are many who still owe him money. But tell me, did any of these people come and meet you and tell you this like your creditors did?'

I had not thought about this point and besides it was of no use to me because my father had left no written record of all these financial transactions.

Talking to Nandu Kaka had helped me. I still hadn't found a solution to my problem but I was now more confident, sure that I would think of some way to solve it.

As I was leaving, Nandu Kaka pushed an envelope into my hands, 'Keep this. Your burden is very heavy but maybe this small gift will help to lighten it in a tiny way.'

I tried to refuse but he insisted, 'Actually, whatever Dhondiba did for me cannot be paid back in money. Please accept this and don't mention it again.'

I couldn't trust myself to speak. I touched his feet and left.

When I reached home and opened the envelope, there were Rs 25,000 in it. Nandu Kaka's helping hand was invaluable to me at that time and I couldn't have treasured it enough!

That night, I could not sleep. There was a battle raging inside me. Until now, I had been a cherished prince. I was in awe of my father's work. I admired his generosity, looked up to him and was proud to be his son. All this had changed in a second. The king was no more and I had to wear his crown. Until this moment I had not realised that the crown had thorns in it and it was so heavy! The question was; would I be happy now that the crown was mine or would I be crushed by the burden of responsibilities it entailed?

The second possibility seemed more real to me at the time. I was an inexperienced, naïve 25 year old. What had I achieved till now? I had graduated, assisted my father in his work, introduced a few minor changes to improve our business; that was about it!

Now, all of a sudden, I was the mukadam of the dabbawalas of Vile Parle, the chief of 25 'lines' (groups) of dabbawalas, responsible for the 1,200 tiffin boxes that they transported. It was now my job to manage all this, from solving disputes between dabbawalas, to increasing the number of clients and seeing that they had no cause to complain.

And as if this was not enough I was also the chief of the entire Medge family. I did have cousins but they said, 'Until now, your father was the head of the family. We are uneducated, ignorant people. You will be the best person for this role.'

Now whether I liked it or not I was responsible for this family of around 40 members. It was up to me to feed them, plan for their school and college education, supervise the farming, maintain the two or three households in different places, see to their health problems, their disputes!

And along with all this, was the additional burden of a debt which amounted to Rs 70,000 or Rs 80,000. I began to feel suffocated. I could not breathe. I tossed and turned and fell into a troubled sleep towards dawn.

In the morning, I could not open my eyes. My head felt heavy, my body listless. When I finally opened my eyes, the whole family was around me. I had a raging temperature.

15

From the Courtroom to the Fields

1980 to 1990, these ten years were extremely trying for young Raghunath Medge. Everyone goes through a difficult patch in life but in the case of Raghunath Medge this period seemed to last a little too long.

The illness that Raghunath suffered from after his father's death continued for a year. The symptoms were strange, not too alarming but at the same time impossible to diagnose. His appetite weakened. He had cold, cough, fever and fatigue. The doctor could not understand if these symptoms were psychological or due to some physical ailment.

Finally, Raghunath decided to begin working in spite of his illness. He had only one aim in mind, 'Increase his income to such an extent that he would be able to look after his entire family of 40 odd members.'

As a mukadam of the dabbawalas in Vile Parle, he was already earning quite well and this business was well settled.

So he decided to concentrate on other avenues which would help him increase his earnings.

One of these was the 'rickshaw'. He got a loan from the bank and bought a rickshaw for Rs 16,000. He obtained a rickshaw driving licence and began driving a rickshaw. He was making a good amount of money.

Some young dabbawalas followed in his footsteps and decided to become rickshaw-walas. They felt it would be a better career option than lugging around 75 kgs of tiffin boxes every day all over the city. Driving a rickshaw would be easier and more profitable. Raghu, being as philanthropic as his father, helped around 80 to 90 young men to procure a rickshaw licence.

Raghunath's brother-in-law, Mr Thopte, gave him moral and at times even financial support.

Raghunath now rented out his rickshaw and having made arrangements to ensure a reasonable income from his business in Mumbai, went to stay in the village.

There, he fell sick once again. There was a whole crop of problems in the village, which showed no signs of dying down, so Raghunath stayed on indefinitely in the village. He would come to Mumbai very rarely, only if it was really necessary for him to do so.

All his fancy dreams had amounted to nothing. The rosy picture he had imagined, of himself wearing an advocate's black gown, had turned into ashes and he was instead reduced to toiling unceasingly under the hot sun, in the fields.

The family owned 32 acres of land, most of which were orchards with mango trees, orange trees and banana trees,

Raghunath brought in his usual innovations here too and very soon, they started growing a variety of crops such as sugar-cane, ground-nuts, onions, coriander, tomatoes, etc.

There are several kinds of loans, subsidies available to the farmer. Raghunath found out everything about these loans and subsidies and utilised them to the utmost.

Raghunath used to work like a man possessed. He bought Jersey cows and ventured in to dairy farming, he took the benefit of a subsidy and started a gobar-gas plant and opened a fertilizer shop. As a means of assuring some income in his village of Avadar, he started a flour-mill there.

He was on a business expanding spree! He would launch into a new venture, perfect its functioning and then move on to the next venture, having transferred the responsibility of running it to a cousin or an uncle.

Soon enough, Raghunath was being aided by several able hands of the family. Thanks to his iniative and drive, more members of his family started working, the family income increased and gradually their problems started decreasing.

Raghunath was just about to heave a sigh of relief, when a dam was built close to the village of Kadus and . . . 12 acres of land and all the property on it belonging to the Medge family, was submerged by the dam.

Building dams is an important feature of progress. However, the farmer, through whose lands the water flows, is devastated by this progress. This is what fate had in store for Raghunath. He received Rs 1.25 lakh from the government as compensation but once again, it was back to square one. He bought new land, built a house on it, installed a pipe-line for water and started farming once again.

Raghunath was making progress, in fits and starts in the field of farming. He did not have the time to personally supervise the dabbawalas and the rickshaw businesses in Mumbai but he was assured of a fixed and steady income from these two sources. It left him free to tackle the problems in farming.

Raghunath took a courageous decision. He bought a tractor. This time too, his brother-in-law helped him out and Raghunath also took a loan from the bank.

The tractor helped Raghunath in two ways; for one, it benefited the farming and for another, it gave him a certain standing in the village. He was now the proud owner of a tractor. It did wonders for his ego and his image in the village. He became more confident and self-assured. He soon came to be known as 'Raghu Seth' in the village. However, just when a man begins to feel relaxed and confident about his future, fate deals him a blow and brings him back to the ground. Raghunath gradually realised that the tractor was a white elephant. The annual instalment on the tractor was Rs 55,000, added to this was the driver's salary, the high maintenance costs. It was a very costly affair. To make matters worse, one day the driver got drunk and landed the tractor in a ditch. It was the last straw! Raghunath decided to give it out on rent.

The tractor issue had soured things between Raghunath and his brother-in-law, who had refused to help him out this time and declared he had nothing to do with the losses incurred because of the tractor. Raghunath tried to reason with him, 'We have shared the profits on the tractor until now, so why should I be the only one to bear the losses?'

However, Mr Thopte was not convinced and they were not on speaking terms for a long time after that incident. There are some periods in a man's life where everything seems to be working against him.

Raghunath's decision to give out the tractor on rent had been a practical and sensible one. Initially, things were fine, however, the money people owed them started piling up. It was the same situation at the fertilizer shop in the village. Raghunath took stock of the situation and found out that the sum owed to them came up to a whopping Rs 2 lakhs! He had to analyse the problem and find out the reason for it. He thought to himself, 'Why is this happening? There are so many Gujarati and Marwari traders in the village who follow the principle of "Cash today, credit tomorrow!" and they are always paid in cash. So why don't people pay us in cash?'

The reason was that all the customers were either friends or relatives or neighbours. We Maharashtrians cannot say 'no'. If we behave sternly, it might spoil our relations, but on the other hand, if we say nothing, we are doomed. Our own people will contribute to our downfall.

Raghunath decided to run the business with a new principle, 'there would be no more friends, relatives, neighbours in business, there would be only customers, who would pay in cash. Giving things on credit was going to be a thing of the past.'

There was a hollow ring to the title, 'Raghu Seth'. He promised himself that he would never again be taken in by superficial things like these.

Raghunath became strict and severe in his business dealings

as he had decided. The villagers were shocked and enraged but they soon realised that this time he meant business and paid up. Once things were on an even keel in the village, Raghunath took another momentous decision, that of returning to Mumbai.

From 1980 to 1990, Raghunath had devoted himself totally to the uplift of his family. He had opened up new pathways for every member of the family and taken great pains to ensure a secure means of livelihood for each person. However, he now realised that as long as he stayed here with them, they would not become completely independent and self-sufficient. They would continue to rely on him. It was now time for them to stand on their own feet.

Raghunath called a meeting of the entire family, 'For the last ten years, I have shouldered the responsibility of the family. But it is now your turn to take on the responsibility. It is now entirely up to you to manage the farming, the tractor, the shops.'

Initially, it was a great shock to the family but they understood his point of view and decided to give it their best.

Ten years after he had left Mumbai, Raghunath decided to return to the city with his wife and three children. It was not going to be an easy task to settle down once again in Mumbai with a big family. But Raghunath had taken up the challenge and he set out in search of new horizons.

16

Back to My Roots

I came back to Mumbai with a new goal, a new dream. What could I do to fulfil this dream?

Several possibilities suggested themselves to me; I could expand the existing rickskaw business, or I could apply for a job in some office. I had tried my hand at various businesses in the village. That experience might prove handy in setting up a new venture here.

The dabbawalas' business was stable and ran like clockwork, whether I was there or not. So I didn't think of doing anything further in that field. I certainly had no interest whatsoever in becoming the president of the Dabbawalas' Association like my father.

One day, I happened to drop into the Dabbawalas' Association's office in Dadar. The management had changed now but there were still a few of my father's colleagues who were on the committee, Gangaram Talekar, Sopanrao Mare,

Hari Bhau Pawar, Laxman Kadam amongst others. As we spoke, a horrifying picture emerged.

Talekar Kaka was distraught, 'Raghu, after your father's death our business has suffered a lot. We had expected that things would go downhill after Dhondiba left us but nobody imagined that things could be so bad!'

I was dazed, 'What exactly is wrong?'

Slowly the situation became clear to me.

Hari Bhau explained, 'As you know, Ram Bhau Nimbalkar succeeded your father as president of the association and Taksale became the secretary. Nimbalkar has not a single one of your father's qualities, his vision, his strict discipline, his forceful personality. He doesn't know anything of managing the business efficiently, he is not aware of what goes on and he can't connect with the people. He is good-for-nothing, a president in name only. The reins are in the hands of that wily fox, Taksale. He is very clever, cunning and sly. He knows how to butter his own bread. Now, you tell me Raghu, what could be the future of an organisation, which has two people like that at the top?'

I agreed. Talekar continued, 'That is not all. To add to all these woes, there were some other changes during the 80s that were terrible for business, the strike in the cloth mills; the nationalisation of banks; the railway strike; all these events had far-reaching consequences for us dabbawalas. Due to the strike in the cloth-mills, lakhs of employees lost their jobs and we lost lakhs of clients. The banks started working in two shifts, hence many employees started going home for lunch, again affecting our business. And during the railway strike, our business was at a total standstill. The railways are our lifeline. How could we transport the dabbas without the trains? There was a series of problems and we only waited and watched. There was no one who could show us a way to overcome these problems. The result, our business is in doldrums.'

As I listened to him, I felt sad and guilty too. While all these events were devastating the Dabbawalas' Association, I was in the village, looking after my family issues. I was not even aware of the seriousness of the situation.

There was no way we could undo what had happened but I was sure of one thing, this could not go on. I asked, 'What is the present situation?'

The three men looked at one another. Finally Kadam Kaka spoke, 'The present situation? Terrible, to put it mildly! The most important problem is that our dabbawalas are no longer scared of anybody, they feel nothing if they do anything wrong. Several have not paid the membership fee for months! The membership fee for our association is only one rupee per person, per month. Not a huge amount, but when taken together, it comes up to a lot and ensures the functioning of our association. Forget about that, there are other major problems; the rent for our Grant Road office is overdue— Rs 40,000; we have a debt of Rs 5 lakhs; we haven't paid the audit fees, nor last year's taxes. There are no written records. A sum of Rs 75,000 has been borrowed from the Cooperative Credit Society and there are no signs of getting that money back. Even the customers have not been spared. Some dabbawalas have been taking an advance every month and if a customer complains, the dabbawalas are least bothered and stop carrying his dabba. Tell me, Raghu have you heard of such things happening during your father's time?'

'No, no, I can't even imagine it and I can't believe my ears!'

Talekar Kaka burst out, 'Even the office maintenance had not been paid. The bank officials came to recover the amount. Finally our fixed deposits were used to cover that. And the mukadams are going out of control. One mukadam owns up to six "lines" of dabbas. That makes him the virtual king of the area and they are misusing their power and splurging like kings. Some of them have three or even four wives, they drink heavily. Raghu, you may not believe this but nowadays it is said that one who doesn't drink and doesn't offer drinks to others is not fit to be a mukadam. What do you have to say to that?'

Hari Bhau interrupted, 'No, no, listen to the whole story first. It is not yet over. One member of the managing committee has kept his mistress in our dharamshala in Jejuri. What was our intention when we had built these dharamshalas? It was to provide accommodation to the dabbawalas at all the religious places. But this arrogant man plans to take over the dharamshala! And last but not the least, there is groupism among the dabbawalas based on the district they come from. They have started fighting amongst themselves. The fights often turn violent, knives and other weapons are used. They fight on the streets, on the railway platform. They have stabbed one another, even bashed up people on their heads. Tell me, today can we say that we are dabbawalas with pride?'

Pride? I was so stunned that my head was spinning. Does the fact that one able man is no longer there cause so much of trouble? How can a well-established business come to the point of being ruined in a matter of 10 years? I didn't know what to do, what to say.

Talekar Kaka put his hand on my shoulder and said, 'Sorry for being blunt but is it is partly your fault too.'

'My fault?'

'Yes. When your father expired, we all expected you to take over the reins of the business in your hands. You were young, but still well-experienced, and most of all, you were educated. As you know, some other dabbawalas' children are also educated but none of them pursued this profession. You were the only exception. You graduated but even then you were a part of our profession. You even put in a lot of effort to bring about improvements in the way it was run. So, we were confident that you would take over from Dhondiba and make a success of it. But after his death, you went away to the village and had nothing to do with this business for 10 years. The dabbawalas were very angry with you and some even said, "He is not a patch on his father. He can never be as great as his father." Even though we knew why you had left us, we couldn't take your side because there was a grain of truth in what they were saying.'

I was shamefaced. There was silence. Nobody said a word. My mind was in turmoil, 'Who am I? Who should I care about? What is my calling? My duty?' And in an instant, I found an answer to all my questions.

I was, and always would be a dabbawala. My life was here

with them, and I had to work with them. This was my profession and this was my vocation.

In a calm voice, I announced, 'Kaka, I am with you from this moment onwards. Together, we will work towards solving all our problems. And I am sure, with our combined efforts, things will soon change for the better.'

We all saw a glimmer of light in the darkness that threatened to swallow us. We looked at each other. 'We will proceed in the right direction and we will work hard to overcome our problems.' We didn't need to say the words. The light of determination and hope shone in our eyes.

17

A New Campaign for Survival

Once my decision was made, we went ahead with full steam. The first thing we did was to call a meeting of 21 veteran, dedicated and sincere members of the association. I was the 22nd member at the meeting.

During the course of the meeting, we took stock of all the events that had affected our association in the past ten years. There were heated debates on several issues like, what went wrong? Who was responsible? What could be done to undo the wrong? etc.

There were many accusations flung at one another, some arguments and a lot of plain talk. Finally everyone accepted his part of the blame and a list of things to be done was drawn up. A lot of resolutions were made:

- We would learn from our past mistakes and ensure that they would not be repeated.

- The rules and regulations would be made more stringent and strict adherence to them would be expected.
- The customers would get top priority and would be assured of the best possible service.
- The customers should not be given cause to complain.
- Elections for a new management committee should be conducted at the earliest.

These elections were necessary to ensure a better, brighter future for the association. The present ineffective president, the corrupt secretary and some good-for-nothing members of the committee had to be replaced.

We started campaigning for the elections as if we were preparing for battle. Surprisingly, winning the elections proved to be a cakewalk. The shareholders were present in large numbers for the meeting. They voted for us enthusiastically and our new panel was elected with an overwhelming majority. There were no arguments, no disputes, no raised voices. Actually, they must all have been unhappy with the way things were being done by Jundhare and Taksale but nobody had had the guts to say so openly. Now that they saw our dedication, our resolve to improve matters, they supported us whole heartedly.

Hari Bhau Pawar, Gangaram Talekar, Dhondi bhau Chaudhari, Sopanrao Mare, Sambhaji Medge and I, Raghunath Medge, were the new members of the management committee. After the elections, everyone unanimously voted for me as president. A new period in my life had begun!

I decided that a clean-up campaign of the organisation was

essential. There were so many things to clear up that I didn't know where to begin!

Our newly-formed committee assembled to discuss these issues; it was decided that the first thing to be done was to get the dharamshala at Jejuri vacated.

This was a dramatic and 'filmi' story. The then secretary of the Nutan Mumbai Tiffin Box Suppliers' Associaton, Mr Taksale, had installed a lady in the dharamshala at Jejuri. Since she was staying there, the dabbawalas could not avail of the facilities of the dharamshala when they went for religious purposes to Jejuri. Taksale refused to take any heed of the complaints of the dabbawalas and did exactly what he wanted.

To begin with, we sent him an official letter, asking him to vacate the association premises. He must have thrown the letter in the dustbin because even though we sent several other letters and finally a legal notice, there was absolutely no response from his side.

We then decided that we would go to Jejuri and take charge of our property. Taksale was from the town of Jejuri whereas we didn't know a soul there.

We met him and tried to settle the issue amicably. But he wouldn't even listen to us. He started abusing us, swearing and shouting. We too were angry. Tempers flared but Taksale was adamant, 'Do what you can!' and slammed the door shut in our face.

We went to the police station to lodge a complaint. We met the inspector on duty, Palsule, and explained the situation to him. But he turned around and started yelling at us, 'You want to file a complaint! In fact, a complaint has already been filed, against you!'

Taksale had filed a complaint against us the previous day itself, 'These thugs have come from Mumbai to harass and threaten me. Please take notice of my complaint.'

Taksale had some guts!

After the inspector had finished his tirade, we left.

We debated over what could be done now. Suddenly, we thought of Popat Seth. He was a prominent builder in Jejuri now, but he had been a dabbawala earlier. Popat Seth was eager to help us. He suggested that we would have to exert the influence of a high-up official to silence the inspector. We drew up a list of people who could help us. One name came up—Vijay Kolte. At that time, Kolte was the head of the Pune Zilla Parishad. He had a lot of connections in the political circles. We went the same night to Pune, met Mr Kolte, and explained the matter to him. He immediately wrote a letter, addressed to the inspector. We thanked him profusely and went back to Jejuri.

This time, Popat Seth approached the inspector, started talking to him and showed him Mr Kolte's letter. But it did not have the effect we were hoping for. Instead of calming down, the inspector became furious. He twisted Popat Seth's arm and tore up the letter into shreds. He threatened us, 'If I see you around tomorrow, you better watch out!'

We were stunned. We realised that Taksale and the inspector were real rogues and would stop at nothing! We had to think of some miraculous plan.

When we asked around, we found out that the woman was alone at the dharamshala. Taksale had not gone near the place since the last few days. He knew that even if we barged in, we would not misbehave with the lady. We decided to take advantage of this 'confidence' that he had placed in us and went to meet the lady.

It was evening. The lady got scared when she saw all of us. But we reassured her, 'Please don't get scared. We will not harm you in any way. We only want to talk to you. Ma'am, we know it is not your fault. It is Taksale's mistake. He should not have brought you here. This property belongs to our association. If we go to the court, the decision will be in our favour and you will have to vacate the premises. Just imagine how demeaning it will be; the bailiff will come here with the court order and start forcibly evicting you and throwing your things out. If you resist, you will be forcibly thrown out! Now, we are not going to do any of these things. We request you to kindly vacate the premises. We are ready to give you money . . .'

We saw a glitter in her eyes at the very mention of the word, 'money'. We now had her entire attention.

We continued, 'Go back to your village. We will give you some money to buy land there and we will also give you some more money to take care of your miscellaneous expenses.'

She liked the idea very much but she still held out, 'I am alone and a woman at that. How will I manage everything?'

'Don't worry about that. Popat Seth has brought his tempo. We will help you pack your belongings and take you right up to your village.'

We offered her the pile of bank-notes and she couldn't hide her happiness. She accepted the money and we quickly piled all her things into the tempo. As she was about to get into the tempo, Talekar called out to the woman, 'Stop!'

She was surprised and a little scared, 'What now?'

But he offered her a sari, a cloth piece and a coconut, (the traditional mark of respect offered to a married woman) to convey our blessings and best wishes.

Her eyes filed with tears at this unexpected gesture and then she got into the tempo. We took photographs as evidence that she had left willingly. As we saw the tail-lights of the tempo receding, we felt like whooping with joy.

That night, lying down on thin mattresses, in the dharamshala, none of us could sleep. We were so happy, so content. We were replaying all the events in our minds. Just then, we saw a flickering light approaching. Who could it be? And then we understood; it must be Taksale. We were choking with laughter, but we forced ourselves to lie down quietly.

Taksale entered and hesitated. Something was wrong! He held up the lantern and instead of the lady, saw our faces! He was terrified, as if he had seen a ghost, in fact six ghosts!

We could not hold back our laughter any longer and burst out laughing. Taksale wheeled around and took off at top speed! We clapped each other on the back and enjoyed our moment of triumph.

We had won the 'battle' of Jejuri in the true spirit of our Maval ancestors, the brave soldiers who had won many battles for Chatrapati Shivaji.

18

Reorienting Ourselves

The first thing we did after returning to Mumbai was to give a six-month notice to all those employees of the association, who had been lazy and inefficient. They had six months to update and clear their accounts. We retained only Mr Gavde, who was a senior, honest and hard-working employee.

No one likes to take extreme decisions like these but I realised that the only way to improve the functioning of the association was to completely overhaul its working.

If we politely show a dog the door, it is not going to go away. We have to be tough, give it a kick and only then are we rid of it.

The employees, who had been given notice, meekly handed in their accounts and left, their tail between their legs.

At this point, I would like to confess to one of my shortcomings. My personality is totally unlike my father's. I cannot pull up anybody. I do not like to yell and shout when

I am angry and I find it impossible to raise my hand and slap or hit someone. Of course, I do get angry. At such times, if I lose my cool and shout at someone, I feel very upset later on. I don't like arguing, even with friends. And if I ever have to pull up an elderly person, I can't sleep at night. The next day, I invariably apologise to the person, 'Uncle, please don't take it to heart. Whatever I said, was for the good of our association. I am sure you will understand, etc.'

I had not planned on becoming the president of the Tiffin Box Suppliers' Association. But now that I had taken on the responsibility, it was my duty to give it my best. It was necessary to maintain a rigid control and to instil fear and respect in the hearts of the illiterate and simple dabbawalas and this was a daunting task for me.

During my father's tenure, I had seen the strict rein he kept over the dabbawalas. I needed to earn that same respect, the same blind trust and faith if I was to turn the business around.

After giving the matter a lot of thought, I came up with a plan and appealed to Hari Bhau Pawar for help. Hari Bhau Pawar had been my father's colleague. He was a powerful figure. His personality was forceful and strong. The dabbawalas were scared of him, especially when he flew into a rage after drinking. I asked Hari Bhau to be with me all the time. We would change our tactics as the situation demanded. If severity and strictness was needed, I would remain silent and Hari bhau would take over. The minute Hari Bhau glared at the offender and started screaming, even the most aggressive dabbawala became meek and subdued and listened quietly. The dabbawala would admit his mistake and do what he had been told.

Our duo, consisting of Hari Bhau and me, worked wonders. I was polite and humble. He was short-tempered and hot-headed. My plan worked like a charm. For the first time since my father, there was perfect discipline among the dabbawalas. I had created a no-nonsense image for myself and the dabbawalas now, once again, followed the rules and regulations sincerely.

It had taken 10 years for the business to go into doldrums. So it was impossible to turn things around with one wave of the magic wand. It would take time to improve the state of affairs of the business and I accepted that. I continued at my own pace. I knew I was heading in the right direction, but only time would prove me right.

We called for a meeting to discuss the debts and financial problems facing the association. Certain important decisions were taken; the membership fee was raised from Re 1 to Rs 5. We decided that the fees that were pending should be recovered at the earliest and a debt recovery campaign was launched.

Out of the 3,000 odd dabbawalas, only 800 used to pay the membership fees because it was optional. Now even though we had raised the fee to Rs 5, we still managed to collect the fee regularly every month and slowly but steadily increase our reserves in the bank.

Even the dabbawalas were convinced that enforcing discipline was necessary for the association because they too were facing financial problems and several of them were in debt.

It was for the purpose of providing credit on easy terms that we had started a Cooperative Credit Society of the association in 1984. Earlier, the dabbawalas would borrow money from the moneylenders or the Pathans. For a loan of Rs 100, the interest per month used to be Rs 10! So forget about repaying the principal, the dabbawalas used to have a tough time repaying the interest. Finally, when it became impossible to repay the interest and principal, the money lender would take charge of whatever asset the dabbawalas had kept as mortgage.

In 1984, we held a meeting to discuss this problem faced by the dabbawalas.

Mr Chaudhary, who worked with us, was a very clever and astute fellow. He had been a dabbawala but then, he had given the GDC exam and had started working with a Parsi accountant. It was decided that we should introduce our own Cooperative Credit Society of the Tiffin Box Suppliers' Association. Mr Chaudhary took on the entire responsibility, and under his guidance, the Credit Society started functioning in 1984. We used to get loan at 14 per cent interest from the Mumbai Zilla Madhyavarti Bank. We started giving loans at 18 per cent interest to our dabbawalas. The instalments were reasonable too. The dabbawalas were freed from the clutches of the moneylenders.

During this period, I used to be more often in the village and was not a part of the day-to-day functioning of the association but I was happy that we had taken a positive step for the welfare of the dabbawalas. When I began working again in 1990 for the association, I realised that I had been wrong. The Cooperative Credit Society was heavily in debt by then. This was because the dabbawalas who had been very prompt in taking the loans were not so prompt when it came to paying the instalments.

We made a serious effort to recover the money and were successful in recovering Rs 5 lakhs. The Credit Society's functioning came back on an even keel.

We had increased the membership fees, recovered a major part of the loans and streamlined the working of the Credit Society. Now we undertook another important task; legally transferring all the dharamshalas in the name of the Association. The dharamshalas in Jejuri, Alandi were in the name of individuals. Though, it was the association which had spent the money, the land and the buildings were not in its name. Some dharamshalas were in my father's name. The Taksale incident had taught us a lesson. We had established a religious Trust and we transferred the ownership of the dharamshalas to the Trust.

The financial position of the association and consequently, of the dabbawalas too was improving. I now turned my attention to 'customer care'.

Actually, 'the customer is king' had been a traditional principle of our business but in the recent years this principle had been ignored.

I now drew up certain strict rules regarding customer care and enforced them rigorously:

- The customers should always be treated with courtesy and respect

- The customers should be dissuaded from using costly tiffin boxes
- Except in extremely rare cases, the tiffin box should always reach the customer on time
- If a tiffin box was lost during transport, half the cost should be borne by the concerned dabbawala

Each dabbawala was given a written copy of these rules and he had to keep them in his record book.

In addition to this, there were some unwritten rules of conduct which had to be inculcated with repetition and practice.

One such unwritten rule is that the dabbawala who begins carrying a particular customer's tiffin box will do so till the end. Just like a 'pativrata' (dutiful) wife is faithful and serves her husband throughout her life, the dabbawala too will faithfully serve the same customer throughout his life.

Another strict rule was punctuality. The time at which the tiffin box will be picked up, is given by the dabbawala on the very first day. The dabbawala himself should always follow this time and the lunch box too had to be ready at the given time. If the dabbawala is supposed to pick up the lunch box at 9.15 a.m., the dabba should be ready by 9.14 a.m.

'Just wait for a minute Bhayya, I have to season the vegetables.' Excuses like these are not acceptable. A dabbawala does not have even a second to lose. This is because he has to collect 30 tiffins and make sure that they go on the correct trains which run at an interval of three minutes! The time-work- speed ratio is so finely tuned that even a second's delay can upset the entire schedule. This is made clear to the customers at the outset. So, the housewives, who prepare the lunch boxes, are mortally scared of the dabbawala who will always ring the bell at the correct time. The customer too realises the importance of punctuality.

As for the dabbawalas, I had prepared a record sheet of their time management for them.

These records had to be filled up every day. When was the tiffin box picked up, when did it reach the customer, when was it returned; all these details are entered daily. This enables us to pick out an error immediately and the concerned dabbawala is then given a warning.

Respect and courtesy are essential to our business, but at the same time discipline is equally important. This is the work ethic that we inculcated in the dabbawalas. The symbols on the tiffin boxes were now more precise, clear and easily understood by all. We also started writing proverbs and slogans on the crates.

'Hard work is the only option'

'Together, we can make the impossible happen'

'Work is worship'

'Jai Jawan, Jai Kisan'

Some were lines taken from the holy songs or 'abhanga' like, 'Wherever I go, you are with me . . .'

I hold the firm belief that if you see good, hear good, you will do good.

I kept repeating to the dabbawalas, 'My dear fellows, take good care of our business. The dabbawala business is not like a shop, which you can close for some days and reopen again.

It is not like agriculture, where the next rain might assure a good crop. Our business depends on human beings. It is important to maintain good relations with the people. The customer is king. It is because of him that we don't go hungry. So do not get upset, do not lose your cool and do not forget our traditional courtesy. If we don't do our job well, they will search for other alternatives like drivers, servants to deliver their lunch or restaurants and other eating places to eat out. If we don't want this to happen, we have to be on our best behaviour. Try and follow the teachings of the great sadhus and saints who advise patience, calm and control over one's emotions and actions. We read the works of Sant Tukaram and Ramdas, we offer prayers and pujas, all these should not go in vain. We must try and follow their teachings. Our conduct should be such that we can hold our head high and proudly say, "We are dabbawalas".'

As I counselled the dabbawalas, I also reasoned with the mukadams. I tried to persuade them to change their attitude, 'One has to lead by example. Our own behaviour should be correct, clean, open and disciplined.' It was difficult to make them see my point of view because by then they were considered kings in the business. They owned several lines of tiffins, had made lots of money and did exactly what they pleased. But I persevered and finally made them understand that they were also partially responsible for the problems the business was facing. One may not be impressed with words, but when it comes to money, everyone is quick on the uptake. Everyone was convinced that if they did not improve their attitude, the business would be ruined and so they all made a sincere effort to improve. Some wore a religious amulet which forbade them from drinking alcohol, some gave up drinking alcohol altogether. Everyone started following the rules. When one is faced with monetary problems, one has to accept the facts and act accordingly to improve the situation.

Our dabbawala court is convened twice a month. Anyone who has committed a mistake is penalised. If someone is caught drunk on the job, he is fined Rs 500 or Rs 1000. If someone fights or quarrels, a certain amount is deducted from his salary.

'In our court, there is no mercy if you have made a mistake. There is only punishment. This organisation has certain rules and regulations which have to be followed. If you do not follow the system, you will be thrown out.' Once the dabbawalas understood these principles, they meekly toed the line.

Vithal Jundhare was the secretary of the association. Sometimes, he would be exasperated by my persistence, 'Medge, these people are illiterate fools. They will never improve. If you succeed in reforming them, I will give you a pat on the back.'

Luckily Jundhare's words were proved wrong and the day when he actually did give me a pat on the back, is one of the most treasured moments of my life!

19

Now Everyone Is an Owner

The new committee of the Dabbawalas Association, with Mr Raghunath Medge as its president, replaced the old system of mukadam and employee by a cooperative system.

It is interesting to analyse how this change came about. While talking to the dabbawalas, I came across some interesting details.

In 1972, Gangaram Talekar applied for a job in the Central Bank of India. After a successful interview, he got the appointment letter. For an average Marathi man, this would seem like the height of good fortune. Talekar, too, was happy but he was faced with a dilemma, 'What should I do now?'

A job in a bank meant security, an increased standing in society, it could even be a reason of envy. But the question was 'prestige or money?' Talekar had been offered a salary of Rs 175 per month in the bank. However, since he was a mukadam, his monthly income in the dabbawalas' business was between Rs 5,000 and Rs 6,000! Naturally money took precedence over prestige and security and Talekar remains till date a dabbawala. However, the irony is that today, even after 30 years in the profession, Talekar's income still remains the same, approximately Rs 6,000 per month.

How could this be possible?

To put things in a nutshell, this puzzling fact is due to the cooperative policies adopted by the dabbawalas.

In order to clarify this point, it is necessary to go back once again to the year 1972.

During this period, the mukadam system was in force. The customer paid Rs 9 to the dabbawala to transport his tiffin box. The dabbawala who picked up and delivered the tiffin boxes earned between Rs 100 to Rs 125 per month, where as a mukadam, who owned 25 to 30 'lines' of tiffins earned at least Rs 6,000 a month.

Even managers in top companies earned Rs 1,500 or Rs 2,000 at the time. So, a mukadam, with his income of Rs 6,000 was naturally a king in his field and the handful of men who were mukadams certainly behaved like kings.

There used to be a 'durbar' (meeting) every morning and evening at the mukadam's house, with all his 'courtiers' (employees) in attendance. After refreshments, the dabbawalas would start off on their day's work.

The evening session was a busy time; the employees' railway passes, the luggage compartment passes, the repairing of bicycles and crates; all these things had to be seen to. In addition to this, minor complaints, disputes, misbehaviour and its punishment were all addressed during these evening meetings. The punishment could either be a fine or at times, a yelling, a warning or even corporal punishment. If anyone was ill, he was taken to the doctor. The day's work, complaints and problems were reviewed the very same day. Nothing was left for the morrow. Everyone would begin the new day with a clean slate. And the session always ended with the much-awaited refreshments, and more importantly drinks! The mukdam offered alcohol, the answer to all tensions, to the exhausted dabbawalas. During those days, it was considered important, nay, obligatory for the mukadams to offer drinks to the dabbawalas. There used to be one or two mukadams in every suburb of Mumbai. Gangaram Talekar was a young, recent mukadam, where as Dhondiba Medge was a senior, experienced mukadam and also the president of the association.

There were several reasons for the decrease in the business of the dabbawalas in the 1980s. As mentioned earlier, the closing down of the textile mills and the ensuing unemployment of thousands of workers; the change in the working hours of the nationalised banks; and the railway strike were some of the reasons.

In addition to these external factors, there was one reason for which the dabbawalas themselves were responsible; the carelessness and 'couldn't care less' attitude of the young dabbawalas. Earlier, the dabbawalas were totally illiterate and ignorant. And it may be for that very reason that they were more sincere and better disciplined. 'Work is worship' was their motto. They used to do their utmost to ensure that the customer was satisfied and that the lunch box reached him on time. So much so that if one dabbawala was ill or had gone to his village, another dabbawala would willingly take on the responsibility of picking up and delivering his tiffin boxes on time. Thanks to their spirit of cooperation and their dedication, their business ran like clockwork. And of course they had the shining example of a great leader like Dhondiba Medge, a man known for his discipline and devotion to work.

Gradually, the scenario changed. Young dabbawalas who had studied till the seventh or eighth grade (some of them had even studied up to the matric level) joined the profession. Like the workers in other domains, these young dabbawalas, who had recently entered into the profession, were well aware of their rights. They started thinking in terms of a 'union'. At the same time they conveniently overlooked aspects like discipline, dedication, etc. They behaved as they pleased and were bothered neither about the customers, nor about the mukadams. During the wedding season in summer, or during the reaping of the rice crop, these men would go back to their village and disappear for months on end. Both the customers and the mukadams suffered. The mukadams were especially worried, 'Who will replace these dabbawalas daily for such a long time?'

'If the customer loses faith in us, he will go elsewhere.'

The mukadams were really tense. However hard they tried to find a substitute and see to it that the customer did not suffer, there was a slip from time to time. Then they had to face complaints from angry customers. It is difficult to run a business efficiently with substitute workers. On the one hand, the volume of their business had decreased and on the other, they were losing more customers because of the careless attitude of these new dabbawalas. The mukadams were in a fix!

One tends to make more mistakes when one is in trouble. The mukadams decided to increase the money they were charging, since the number of customers had gone down. This infuriated the customers even further and they started looking for other alternatives. The volume of the dabbawalas' business went down even further. The dabbawalas knew they were making the wrong decisions but at that moment, they lacked the guidance of a wise and experienced leader like Dhondiba Medge. Everyone across the lines, from the dabbawalas to the mukadams were in a terrible situation.

'Better late than never'—how true these words are! In 1990, Raghunath Medge became the president of the association. He implemented many changes, introduced and enforced new rules and regulations. Thanks to his initiatives, the functioning of the association gradually started improving. One such novel idea was the introduction of the cooperative principle.

When a shop runs into losses, the shopkeeper often sells it. After 1985, the mukadams started selling their 'lines' of dabbas. Earlier too, the mukadams would sell their 'lines', but normally to other mukadams. Now the mukadams sold their 'lines' to their own employees. Some young, ambitious dabbawalas took loans from the Cooperative Credit Society and started buying 'lines', one at a time. It was like buying a share worth Rupee 1 for Rs 7. For example, a 'line' of tiffin boxes which earned Rs 700 was sold by the mukadams for Rs 5,000.

The important mukadams like Raghunath Medge, Gangaram Talekar, Chaudhary sold several of their 'lines'. Everyone kept one 'line' with them and sold off the rest to their employees. Raghunath gave a few 'lines' to his cousins.

After Independence, there were very few rulers of royal states like the Ruler of Aundh near Pune who voluntarily gave up their kingdom to the Government of India. But for the rest, it needed the extreme measures of the 'Iron Man', Sardar Patel, to make the rulers see reason.

In comparison, one has to admire the pragmatism of the mukadams. These men, kings in their own domain, understood that they had to change with the times. They voluntarily, though not always happily, decided to sell their 'lines' to their employees in order to ensure a better future for themselves.

Today, there are no mukadams in the Tiffin Carrier's business. One man can 'own' only one line of dabbas. For example, in Vile Parle, if there are 11 'lines' of tiffin boxes, there are 11 groups working there, with 11 owners and their dabbawalas. Today, a customer pays Rs 300 or Rs 350 per month to the dabbawala. The dabbawala collects the money from the customer. This money is handed over to his group. The expenses are noted down; these don't normally vary; the usual expenses are the railway passes for the dabbawalas, the passes for the luggage compartment, the repairs of the bicycles and crates. Once the expenses are deducted, the profits are equally distributed among the owner and the dabbawalas.

Everyone earns around Rs 5,500 to Rs 6,000 per month. The figure varies slightly according to the number of tiffin boxes ferried every month. Today, the distinction between the owners and dabbawalas is restricted to the kind of work they do and not the income. Everyone gets an equal share of the profits. That is the reason why Gangaram Talekar earns almost as much as an owner today as he used to earn when he was the mukadam in 1972.

The dabbawalas who had not even heard of Karl Marx, socialism or stock options are shining examples today of a socialist organisation, where everyone is equal. 'Everyone is an owner today!' This is one of the great achievements of the dabbawalas business and also one of the keys to their success.

20

The Mystery of the Six Sigma

It was in the year 2000, I don't remember the month, when two young boys entered our office in Dadar. It was a hot afternoon and the boys seemed exhausted by the heat. They didn't look as if they were from Mumbai.

The boys gulped down a glass of water. They seemed puzzled when they were asked in Marathi, 'Do you want to start sending your tiffin box?'

When I translated the question in Hindi, they shook their heads. 'We have come here to study.'

'Oh! Then you have come to the wrong address. This is not a college.'

They took out an address and asked, 'Is this the office of the Tiffin Box Suppliers' Association, Nav Prabhat Chambers, Third floor, Ranade Road, Dadar(W), Mumbai?'

'The address is correct but you are mistaken, we don't teach anything here.'

'No, no, there is a misunderstanding. We have come here to study you dabbawalas.'

Study us? Now, it was our turn to look puzzled.

The boys explained. They were students of a famous management college in New Delhi. Their principal had sent them to Mumbai to prepare for a project, 'Mumbai's Dabbawalas'.

We now understood why they were here but we still didn't know why they had chosen us, the dabbawalas of Mumbai, as a topic of study. What was so special about us?

When I asked them this question, they were amazed, 'Don't you know?'

When we shook our heads, the boys launched into a detailed explanation.

They talked about things which were totally new to us but what we managed to understand after the lengthy explanation, was, that, there is a very famous Indian man, who lives in America, C.K. Prahlad, who is a 'Management Guru'. He teaches in a university there and is often invited to give lectures in different universities, all over the world. He was recently felicitated in New Delhi, by President K.R. Narayanan. During his acceptance speech, Mr C.K. Prahlad spoke in glowing terms about the dabbawalas of Mumbai, 'When I collected information about the dabbawalas, analysed their working style, I was amazed. I always give their example when I am asked to speak about ideal management principles. I do not know if the dabbawalas are aware of the fact, but in 1998, they were awarded the highly coveted "Six Sigma" performance rating by the prestigious American business publication, *Forbes Global*. This is an honour indeed! Forbes Global accorded the dabbawalas 99.99999 points on the basis of their time management and work efficiency. This has placed the dabbawalas among the exalted ranks of the giant business houses like GE and Motorola . . .'

The CEO of 'Six Sigma' Mr Pradeep Deshpande, another reputed management guru in the United States, always talks highly about the amazing working style of the dabbawalas.

The principal of the management college in New Delhi heard of this and he was also advised by Mr C.K. Prahlad to encourage the students to select the dabbawalas of Mumbai as the topic for their project. He asked the students to research the subject, find out the latest statistics and figures, the logistics of the business. This would most certainly benefit the management students.

That is why these boys had landed up in our office. Now, if you found out all this information about yourself from a third person, wouldn't you be dazed? We were a sensation in America and we didn't know a thing? We had never in our life heard about C.K. Prahlad, Pradeep Deshpande, Six Sigma, Forbes Global! Of course, I didn't reveal all this to the boys and said, 'OK. You go ahead with your project and "study" us. Just tell us what we can do to help you in your research.'

'We only want to be with you and observe the way you work, for a week!'

The boys left but we were worried. How would these boys from Delhi manage to navigate through the Mumbai crowds, get quickly into moving trains? Getting around in Mumbai is difficult for outsiders and to keep pace with the super-fast dabbawalas, who are always running, is next to impossible. The dabbawalas have only a minute to load or unload the crates into the train. Their speed is amazing. How would these boys keep up with them?

Finally we decided to appoint two dabbawalas to take care of the two boys. I gave them detailed instructions, 'These boys are not from Mumbai so they are not as quick as the Mumbaikars. Take care of them. We don't want anything untoward to happen.'

For a week, the boys covered the entire length and breadth of the city with the dabbawalas, from Virar to Churchgate and from VT to Kalyan. They spoke to a lot of dabbawalas and their clients. They also met the members of the managing committee. The boys were curious and eager to learn all they could and fired questions at us. One of them asked, 'You say that all the dabbawalas are shareholders but I didn't find a single thing in writing about this in your papers.'

I smiled, 'Ours is not some manufacturing company, with printed registered share certificates. The shares that we talk about, are in our hearts and minds. We have a very simple definition of the word, share. Whatever we earn collectively, has to be divided equally amongst all of us. Our great Indian culture teaches us to divide a sesame seed among seven people. The same values are seen in the *Mahabharata*, when the Pandavas were asked by their mother to divide whatever they had got equally among themselves and in this way Draupadi got five husbands. It is inscribed in our minds that we all are shareholders and everyone has an equal share in the business. So we do not need to waste paper, files, etc., to provide proof of the fact.'

When the boys heard this definition of shareholdings, they were stunned and noted every little detail in their notebooks.

Their next question was, 'The whole world is run by computers today. Your business activities are so complex! Do you take the help of computers to manage them?'

Gangaram Talekar replied, 'How is a computer going to help us in our business? See, we dabbawalas are the means by which the food prepared by the housewives at home reaches the office-goers in their offices. Now tell me, will the computer prepare the food or deliver it? But yes, all of us are equipped with one computer each, our brain! All the details are fed into this "computer" of ours: where is the tiffin box to be picked up from, at which station does it have to be unloaded from the train, which office does it have to be delivered to, etc. All we use, to protect this computer of ours, is our favourite Gandhi cap! Our computer functions non-stop, in all seasons and always to perfection!'

The boys found it difficult to believe, 'You say that the system works to perfection. But there must be problems cropping up; an accident, a theft or a fraud. Something must be going wrong sometimes!'

I replied, 'We are only human and errors do happen. And like you say, there are accidents sometimes. When a man is climbing into or getting down from a crowded train with 70 kgs of weight on his head, he slips sometimes. If he is not seriously hurt, he just carries on as if nothing has happened and delivers the tiffins to his clients on time. He sees to his injuries in the evening, after his day's work is done. If the injuries are serious, then another dabbawala takes the injured man to the hospital, while a third dabbawala takes over and delivers the tiffin boxes on time. The client is not even aware that an accident has taken place. We always have two or three extra dabbawalas on duty to handle emergencies like these because at all costs, the tiffin box has to reach the client as scheduled. Like the 12th player in the cricket team, we too have a substitute "player" to take over the duty if there are unexpected emergencies.

'Now about thefts, there are a few rare incidents which do take place. It happens like this: the dabbawala enters a building with the tiffin boxes on his bicycle or in the crate. He can't possibly take either the cycle or the crate upstairs so he asks the watchman or the paanwala on the road to keep an eye on his cycle or crate and goes up to pick up or deliver the tiffin box. Normally, nothing happens. But in a rare case, a passing beggar or hungry soul steals a tiffin box. In such a case, the dabbawala first apologises to his client. In the evening, he makes a trip to Chor Bazaar and usually finds the same tiffin box being sold there. He buys it and returns it to the client. In case he does not find the tiffin box, he gives money as compensation to the client and the matter ends there.

'As to fraud, tell me, where is the scope for fraud? It is almost impossible that a dabbawala eats the client's tiffin, for example. There are two reasons for this: firstly he would incur the wrath of the client and secondly, if it came to our notice, he would lose his job. Who would want to risk his job for such a small thing? Normally, the dabbawalas, after having delivered their clients' tiffins, open their own tiffins and have lunch. A simple meal: either rotis with some vegetable or bhakri(a kind of roti) with chutney or sometimes just bhakri and an onion! The onion is crushed with their fist and eaten raw.'

The boys got all the material they wanted in a week. They clicked photos and even made a film. After returning to their institute, they completed their project and sent us a letter thanking us for our help.

Many months passed. We had even forgotten about this incident, when we received a call from one of the boys who had done the project, 'Medge Sir, have you heard?'

'Heard what?'

'*India Today* has published an article on you! They too must have heard of the Six Sigma certification which you were awarded by *Forbes Global*. They have given all those details and praised you warmly!'

Once again, I was stunned. A famous publication in India carries an article on us and we know nothing about it. If I said so, we would look like ignorant fools. What could I say? At the same time I couldn't find words to express my joy and happiness. So I thanked him and finally I couldn't help myself from asking, 'Can we see the magazine?'

'Of course! It is in the June 2001 issue. One of my friends is coming to Mumbai. I will send it with him. Congratulations, once again!'

The very same evening, his friend from New Delhi met me at Jal Computer Centre, near the Santacruz Airport and gave me a copy of the magazine.

I read the article about the dabbawalas of Mumbai. After giving all the statistics and other details about our business, they quoted from the report of Forbes Global 'The dabbawalas from Mumbai make only one single error in 60 lakh human transactions! That is why we are awarding them the Six Sigma performance rating!'

As I read the words, my hand trembled and my eyes misted over!

21

What Is the Six Sigma?

These days one often hears the term 'Six Sigma' but many of us are not sure of what it exactly means. So let us try and understand this concept!

To put it in a nutshell, Six Sigma can be the key to success. It refers to a behavioural concept or approach which can be adapted to suit any domain.

The Six Sigma can prove to be extremely useful not only in giant business ventures but also in small and medium scale industries, organisations, banks or even for managing our household work or finances.

The president of the Six Sigma and Advanced Control Company in the United States of America, Mr Pradeep Deshpande says, 'I used the Six Sigma system while planning my son's wedding! Thanks to this system, I was happy that the wedding arrangements were the best that we could have made.'

In 1980, the Motorola Incorporated began practising the Six Sigma and made it popular.

Thanks to the Six Sigma concept, several objectives were successfully achieved:

- Increase in the company's production and improvement in the quality of its products
- Enhanced customer satisfaction with regards to the products
- Enlargement of the customer base
- Growth in the scope of the company's activities
- Increase in profits

GE, another business giant in the United States of America, followed the example of Motorola and adopted the Six Sigma approach. This successful company became even bigger and more successful, thanks to the Six Sigma!

Six Sigma then became the key word and business houses fell over themselves to join the bandwagon.

Now to come back to the concept of the Six Sigma; there is a contradiction in the very name itself. Six Sigma refers to FIVE (and not six) steps of the ladder of success! These five steps are: Define, Measure, Analyse, Improve and Control or in short DMAIC. Once these steps are taken, the success that one achieves is measured in a different way. The criteria for success here are: customer satisfaction, time saved, monetary profits, increase in size and improved efficiency.

Following the ideal of Motorola and GE, several business houses, both big and small, started implementing the Six Sigma principle. In fact, this principle proved extremely successful in the service sector as well, for example in the banking sector and hundreds of thousands of people benefited from it.

To understand where and how the Six Sigma can be used, let us take the example of a bank, XYZ Bank, which begins implementing the Six Sigma.

1. *Define:* The first task is to define what can be done to provide the utmost satisfaction to the bank's customers. For example: opening an account easily, increasing the speed of functioning by installing teller windows, providing facilities like the ATM, giving loans on easy instalments, etc.

2. *Measure:* The second task is to see how much more satisfied the customer is because of the new ideas introduced. One cannot measure satisfaction, happiness, etc., in metres or inches. To do that, one has to initiate a dialogue with the customers, ask for their opinions and keep their suggestions in mind when introducing any change.

3. *Analyse:* At this step, self-evaluation is necessary. Are the customers getting better service now? Is their time saved? Self analysis and self introspection is required at this stage.

4. *Improve:* Even if the system of working is excellent, some errors do occur while it is being implemented. One had to take into consideration the customer's complaints and queries. One has to find solutions and answers to these complaints and queries and more importantly,

evaluate the solutions. If there is something amiss, one has to reinvent oneself and rectify the errors. The ultimate goal should be: 'The complete satisfaction of the customer' and one should always try out new ways to accomplish this goal.

5. *Control:* There has to be constant monitoring of the steps taken to increase customer satisfaction and to see that the changes are being implemented correctly.

If the right balance is struck between the following factors: customer satisfaction, the money spent for it, the increase in staff and other expenses, and the increase in the bank's profit; then one can say that one has successfully implemented the Six Sigma principle.

If a company has successfully implemented the Six Sigma and thus increased its growth and profit, it is internationally acclaimed. Every year, a list of those who have received this performance rating, is published in the 'Forbes Global' business magazine.

The companies usually vie with one another to be included in this select list. It is indeed ironical that the dabbawalas, who were not even aware of something called the Six Sigma, received the coveted rating. A similar case has never occurred before this. That is why the dabbawalas are of special significance.

Generation after generation of dabbawalas worked devotedly, evaluated themselves continuously and constantly searched for new, improved methods to serve their customers. For them, the customer was king, and delivering his lunch to him on time was their ultimate goal. These were the simple principles of these dedicated men. Their unceasing efforts to improve themselves led to a 100 per cent effective time management, minimal human errors and the satisfaction and confidence of their clients.

That is why the dabbawalas today find themselves in the same category as GE or Motorola. And objectively speaking, the dabbawalas are, in fact, the most deserving of the three. This is because the dabbawalas have achieved this glory in spite of being ignorant and illiterate, in spite of having no financial or technical background. What they do have is dedication to their work and faith in humanity. We salute these incredible men!

22

Prince Charles Meets the Dabbawalas

The *Forbes Global* business magazine announced that we had received the Six Sigma certification and that our organisation was now part of a small select group of companies (though ours was not a company actually) in the world. We were very pleased by this news but it did not make even the slightest difference in our hectic life. Firstly, nobody in Mumbai was aware of this news and even if they had been, I am not sure how much of importance they would have given it!

To tell you the truth, though we were very happy with our achievement, we didn't shout it from the rooftops. We didn't feel we had accomplished something great.

When I became the president of the Tiffin Box Suppliers' Association, my only objective was to try and revive the dying business, to provide a steady and reasonable income to the dabbawalas and their families and to improve our future.

When I started out on my mission in 1990, this task seemed almost impossible. Gradually, after continued efforts, I felt that we were inching forward towards our goal. In the last few years, I had felt that things were definitely changing for the better. Now, thanks to the Six Sigma rating that we had received, I was confident and satisfied that I had achieved my objectives to some extent.

It was the month of August 2003. It was raining heavily. Many office-goers had stayed at home fearing that the trains might stop working. But for us, it was work as usual since we had to deliver the tiffin boxes to those who had gone to office. The dabbawalas, drenched to the skin, were loading and unloading the tiffin boxes from the trains as usual.

I too was drenched by the time I reached our office in Dadar. As I entered, the phone was ringing. Without waiting to dry myself, I picked up the receiver, water streaming down my hand.

'Namaste. My name is Jeetendra Jain. I work at the British High Commission. May I speak to Mr Raghunath Medge please?'

'Speaking. How may I help you, Sir.'

'Medge Saheb, first of all, allow me to congratulate you. Mr Medge, the dabbawalas are in news all over the world. You have been awarded the Six Sigma performance rating by *Forbes Global* magazine, *Time* magazine has published and article on you and there was a story on your organisation on the BBC channel.'

'Yes, some management students did tell us about the Six Sigma and about the article in *India Today* as well. But that was some time ago.'

'Prince Charles saw the film on you on BBC and was highly impressed. He would like to meet you.'

I couldn't trust myself to speak. The prince of England wanting to meet us dabbawalas! What could we say to him and how? Mr Jain must have guessed what I was thinking so he said, 'Prince Charles is coming to Mumbai in the first week of November. We will decide on the day, time and venue of the meeting according to his schedule and your convenience. Will that be all right?'

I accepted.

Mr Jain continued, 'I will call you next week and we can discuss the matter in detail. Thank you very much.'

I was so dazed that I clutched the receiver in my hand even after the call had ended. 'Was this all true or was someone pulling my leg?' Well, we would find out soon enough.

But the following week, Mr Jain called again, as he had promised. We talked several times during the ensuing weeks.

It was decided that Prince Charles would meet the dabbawalas in Mumbai on 4 November. Now the other details to be decided were: Where should the meeting take place and what should be the duration of the meeting.

I announced at the very beginning, '4 November being a working day, it would not be possible for the dabbawalas to go somewhere to meet the prince. But of course, if he came to their place of work, they would be delighted and honoured to meet him.'

This suggestion was accepted. It was decided that Prince Charles would come to Churchgate railway station, where the sorting of tiffin boxes took place, and would meet the dabbawalas for 15 minutes.

We too called a meeting of our committee members. The main topic on the agenda was: How should we welcome the prince when he comes to meet us?

All the details were discussed and finalised.

'Prince Charles is going to meet the dabbawalas during his trip to Mumbai' This news was announced to the media by the British High Commission.

The initial reaction was surprise and amazement. Why was the prince interested in meeting the dabbawalas?

When the media found out the details, it was like an instant revelation. Until yesterday, we were one among the anonymous crowds of Mumbai. Now, all of a sudden, we were encircled by a glorious halo!

There was frenzy in the media! Articles were written, interviews were aired on radio and television, flashbulbs were being popped day and night!

- Prince Charles to meet the Dabbawalas
- The Dabbawalas of Mumbai: a miraculous story
- Prince Charles enthralled by the Dabbawalas' story
- Prince Charles and the Management Gurus—the Dabbawalas of Mumbai

Articles about us made the headlines on the front page of all major Marathi, Hindi and English newspapers. I won't deny it, we were thrilled with all the attention! The spotlight on us warmed our heart. It was like a dream come true.

There were unending formalities to be completed before we met the prince. First of all, we were asked to submit a list of the names and addresses of the six persons who would be meeting Prince Charles. Then we were thoroughly investigated by the CID to verify our background and to confirm that none of us had any criminal record. We were then issued photo-passes.

We received a message from the High Commission, 'The Prince would like to see the tiffin boxes that you carry, as well as the crates, baskets, etc., that you transport them in.'

We said, 'The tiffin boxes belong to our clients. We cannot open them. But we will bring a special tiffin box for the prince.'

The 'dabba' or tiffin box had a very important role to play in our meeting with Prince Charles, so we decided to buy a brand new dabba for the occasion. Now the question arose, 'How could we show an empty tiffin box to the prince?'

It was decided that we would fill the lunch box with our special traditional food. We finalised the menu: Gulab jamun, masala rice, rotis, vegetables, etc.

I personally supervised the making of a new wooden basket which is used to carry the tiffin boxes and had it painted white.

Right from the stage, to the main actors, to the property; everything was being readied for the dramatic meeting!

Finally 4 November, the auspicious day of Kartiki Ekadashi according to the Hindu calendar, dawned. For a week now, the entire media had been talking about Prince Charles meeting the dabbawalas in front of Churchgate station at 11 o'clock. At the appointed time, there was a huge crowd of around two hundred dabbawalas and thousands of Mumbaikars outside Churchgate station. And of course, the journalists, photographers, television reporters and their crew were there in full strength too.

After taking stock of the situation, the police decided that there would be a minor change in the venue. Instead of meeting on the pavement outside the station, Prince Charles would now meet us inside a small building compound. The area was first sniffed and checked by the dog squad.

Finally, the most eagerly awaited moment arrived! The impressive Land Rover, bearing the flag of the Prince of Wales stopped in front of the station, closely followed by half a dozen other cars from the British High Commission.

Prince Charles, wearing a dark blue suit, got down from the car and was whisked into the compound by the security personnel. Six of us—Gangaram Talekar, Sopanrao Mare, Dhondiba Chaudhary, Damodar Pingle, Rohidas Adhav and me—dressed in our typical dabbawala's uniform of white pyjama, white shirt and white Gandhi cap, were waiting to greet the prince. We joined our hands in the traditional Indian greeting and stepped forward to greet the prince.

Prince Charles put out his hand and shook hands with all of us. We garlanded him and then the conversation began. The British High Commission had provided us with an interpreter, so there would be no problem in communicating with the prince.

There was admiration and appreciation in Prince Charles's glance, 'I read the article "Dabbawalas of Bombay" in *Time* magazine and I also saw the film aired on BBC about you and I was fascinated! Since then, I have been wanting to meet you and learn more about your work.'

And then followed a series of questions! The prince was so curious and eager to know more about us and our work.

- How many dabbawalas work in Mumbai?
- How many tiffin boxes do you transport every day?
- How come there are minimal errors in your work?
- What do the symbols on the tiffin boxes mean? etc . . .

We were doing our best to reply to all his questions.

We showed him the tiffin box that we had got for him and also the crate filled with 35 tiffin boxes.

Prince Charles asked us, 'How much does this crate weigh?' '70 to 75 kgs.'

He was extremely surprised to hear the figure, 'You walk, climb into trains and get down from the trains with such a heavy load on your head. Doesn't that lead to a strain on your neck and back?'

To tell you the truth, the very fact that he had asked us this question meant so much to us! This profession has been in existence for the past 110 years! But nobody had cared enough to ask us this question! We were touched that this question came from an Englishman who had given so much of thought to us and our problems.

He was especially amazed by the fact that the majority of dabbawalas were illiterate and that they still managed to do their job with such great efficiency and zero errors. As Gangaram Talekar said, 'The Mumbai train might run late but our dabbawalas ensure that the tiffin always reaches the client on time!'

We tried to give as much information as possible, about

our profession to the prince during this 15 minute meeting. He looked at us with admiration and surprise and commented spontaneously, 'I must say, that your organisation, which assures such excellent service at such a low cost, is indeed unique! It is amazing!'

The meeting was coming to an end, so we proffered the tiffin box that we had got for Prince Charles. When he opened it, I explained, 'This is the traditional Indian lunch of roti and vegetable that we deliver to our clients.'

I requested him, 'Won't you please do us the honour of tasting it?'

He tasted a few dishes and then asked us, 'Won't you please have something too?'

I thanked him and said, 'Today, most of us are fasting on the auspicious occasion on Kartiki Ekadashi. We are all followers of the Lord Vithoba of Pandharpur and today is a holy day for us. Most of us also wear a religious chain around the neck, so we are vegetarians and we don't drink alcohol. We also observe a lot of fasts.'

All this was new and interesting for the prince.

Before bidding him goodbye, we presented him with a shawl, a coconut, mementos with the images of Sant Dnyaneshwar and a tiffin box, and also a Gandhi cap.

We had heard that during a ceremony in his honour in Rajasthan, Prince Charles had worn the traditional 'pagdi', so we requested him to put on the Gandhi cap. The prince accepted all our gifts and expressed his appreciation. However, he politely declined to wear the Gandhi cap and put it instead, in his coat pocket, 'I will take this cap with me as a souvenir from you and I will keep it in my collection back home. Thank you.'

The media persons had come forward, thinking that the prince would wear the cap and they were disappointed when he did not do so.

Before leaving, Prince Charles asked us, 'What can I do to help you?'

I replied, 'We want your blessings, that is all. We are more than happy with the love and concern you have shown and we thank you from the bottom of our heart.'

Prince Charles turned to go and then, putting aside all security concerns, he went out and mixed freely with the dabbawalas who were waiting outside. There are only three women among the 5,000 Mumbai dabbawalas. One of them, Dagdabai Adhav was waiting in the crowd. Prince Charles went towards her, talked to her and pointing to a nearby crate, asked, 'How do you carry such a heavy crate on your head?'

Dagdabai smiled and in one gesture lifted the heavy 75 kg crate on to her head and said to the prince, 'Like this!'

Everyone burst out laughing and the meeting came to an end.

We felt like Lord Vithoba himself, but a fairer version of him, had come to see us on this holy day of Kartiki Ekadashi!

It was an unforgettable experience for all of us!

23

Management Guru Number 1

The minute that it was known that Prince Charles would meet the dabbawalas in Mumbai, the media had discovered a new hero! The dabbawalas!

Prince Charles and the dabbawalas represent two diametrically opposite sides of a spectrum. The prince of England, the country which had ruled over India for 150 years, was going out of his way to meet the dabbawalas, whose ancestor Mahadu Bacche had started the whole enterprise while the British were still ruling India! And why was the prince so eager to meet the dabbawalas? To learn more about their business and the secret of their efficient management.

This was a juicy story and the media made the most of it. Newspapers, television programmes were full of the topic even before the actual meeting could take place.

On the day of the meeting, there was tremendous

excitement because everyone knew that the dabbawalas would be offering a Gandhi cap to Prince Charles. The episode had all the makings of high drama. The cap, named after Mahatma Gandhi, who had been referred to as 'nanga fakir' in England, (and who incidentally never wore the Gandhi cap) might be worn by the prince of the very same country! It promised to be a historical moment.

The media was all set to click photographs of Prince Charles wearing a Gandhi cap . . . but what a disappointment!

The Prince graciously accepted the gift but did not wear it. He put it in his pocket and promised to keep it as a part of his personal collection.

But it is the media's role to create news! So this simple gesture was now given a new implication and there was a spate of headlines like:

- Insult!
- Dabbawalas insulted
- Insult of the Gandhi cap

Raghunath Medge put a decisive end to the controversy, 'We are more than happy and honoured that Prince Charles accepted our gift. In no way were we or the Gandhi cap humiliated. We have nothing to do with politics and never will. So this should not be given any political overtones and should not be used as a pretext by the politicians to further their own cause!'

Now that the Gandhi cap incident had turned out to be a damp squib, the media focused on another issue.

Professor John of the JJ School of Arts had sculpted a

life-size statue of the dabbawalas, which was exhibited in an exhibition at the Yashwantrao Chavan Auditorium. One politician came up with the idea that this statue should be presented to the dabbawalas, who would then in turn, present it to the prince. Actually, of what use would the statue be to the prince. But politicians do not ask themselves such questions!

Prince Charles politely refused to carry the statue back to England. Now this was a new controversy, 'Prince Charles lauded the efforts of the dabbawalas but the weight of one dabbawala proved too much for him!'

Anything related to the dabbawalas made the headlines and the Press persisted in finding more material as long as the fervour lasted. On the other hand, the publicity proved beneficial to the dabbawalas because the common man in Mumbai was now aware of their achievements. Everyone, from the ordinary citizen to a millionaire was curious and eager to know more about the dabbawalas and their work.

Not even huge business houses had got this kind of recognition abroad or in reputed international magazines. So why were these simple, illiterate people being singled out? Everyone wanted to know the answer to this question.

A series of invitations followed. Most of the major management institutes in India contacted the dabbawalas and invited them.

The invitations were for lectures, interviews, discussions, symposiums . . . But whatever the title, the aim was the same, 'to find out the secret of their success'.

When I started meeting the dabbawalas, I observed that

their annual planner was choc a bloc with appointments. They constantly received phone calls inviting them, or well-dressed visitors with invitation cards in their hand.

Raghunath Medge and Gangaram Talekar had already given lectures in several prestigious management institutes in New Delhi, Bangalore, Goa, Ahmedabad, etc.

I too was eager to hear these new 'management gurus' speak, to watch their demonstration and I soon had the opportunity to do so.

The reputed NMIMS in Mumbai had organised a special two-day seminar and had invited management gurus from all over India, the dabbawalas being one of them.

At the appointed time, I entered the auditorium of the NMIMS. The auditorium was spacious, luxurious, ultra-modern and extremely impressive. Everything from the rich carpeting to the well-appointed seats bespoke style and elegance. The colour coordination and the ambiance being western, one had the impression of being in Europe or America.

The persons present also complemented the western, intellectual and elegant ambiance: students of the management school, faculty members, some noted businessmen and reporters; all highly educated and cultured. Everyone was formally attired in suits, or was wearing at least a formal tie. The fragrance of expensive, designer perfumes lingered in the air. All around me, I could hear excellent English, spoken with an impeccable accent. Even a middle-class man would have felt out of place in such a setting but our simple dabbawalas seemed totally at ease. Anyone who saw the dabbawalas sitting amongst the other reputed orators would have been astounded. They might have asked themselves what these men, who would have been more at home in a vegetable market or a gram panchayat office, were doing in this august gathering.

I started feeling tense on their behalf! The first speaker, Professor Dr R.S.S. Mani, stood up and began his speech on 'The new techniques of management'. Professor Dr Mani was a renowned orator, who had toured the globe giving speeches on this topic. Because of his mastery over the English language, his sense of humour and his extensive knowledge of the subject, his speech enthralled the audience. He had a repertoire of amusing anecdotes and interesting quotations; for example:

'Those who can . . . do,

Those who can't . . . teach,

And those who can't do both the things . . . do consultancy.

Which I do!

So those who can do business . . . do exactly that,

Those who can't . . . teach it

And those who can't do both these things . . . work as consultants,

Like I do!'

This was greeted with laughter and applause from the audience.

Prof Dr Mani explained the innovative and modern techniques that businessmen could implement in the 21st century. He complemented his words with slides projected from his laptop and provided extremely valuable and relevant information. When Prof Dr Mani's lecture demonstration came to an end, everyone in the audience had the feeling of having learnt a valuable lesson and they applauded him enthusiastically.

It was now the turn of Mumbai's dabbawalas to address the audience.

Instead of them, it was me, who had butterflies in my stomach. I was wondering how this intellectual audience would react to them after Prof Dr Mani's impressive performance.

The master of ceremonies gave an introduction of their work and achievements. There was thunderous applause at the very mention of the magic words, 'Six Sigma', and the applause was repeated at the mention of the article in the *Time* magazine, the story on BBC, the mention in *Guiness Book of World Records* and *Ripley's 'Believe it or not!'*

I didn't even realise when I had stopped holding my breath! These brave men from Maval had won the war before the start of the first battle. After the introduction was over, Gangaram Talekar stood up to speak amid pin-drop silence, 'Hame Angrezi nahi ati, to mai Hindi me bolnewala hun.' Even the Hindi that Gangaram Talekar was speaking was identifiable as that language only because of the 'hai' at the end of each sentence. Otherwise, his Hindi had a decidedly Marathi flavour to it!

I stole a glance at the audience. Nobody seemed to be paying the least bit of attention to the peculiarity of his language, everyone was eager to learn about the amazing working system of the dabbawalas. Gradually, all the impediments of language, education and sophistication melted away and the audience became a part of the incredible world of the dabbawalas.

With an invocation to Sant Dnyaneshwar, Talekar began to recount the dabbawalas' prodigious journey from the arrival of Mahadu Bachhe in Mumbai. In simple words, he narrated the story of the dabbawalas' success. He knew exactly what to say, what points to emphasise and how to captivate his audience. During his 20-minute speech, he explained the culture of the dabbawalas, their working system, their ideas and principles, their problems, their attitude towards life and work. His humour, wit and simplicity mesmerised the audience. Here are some excerpts from his speech:

'Hum sab dabbewale Thums Up company ke log hain! . . . matlab (a dramatic pause) Angootha Chaap!'—We dabbawalas all belong to the Thums Up company, that is we are all illiterate and most of us cannot even sign our names.

'Hum sushikshit (educated) nahi hain, isiliye hum apne mendu pe (brain) bharosa karte hain aur iska puri taraha se istamal karte hain!'—Since we are not educated, we rely on our brain and utilise it to the utmost.

'Hum logon ko lunch ka dabba pahunchate hain, isliye time management ka pura dhyan rakhte hain. Ek minute ki deri ho gayi to samajhte hain, ho gaya pura satyanash. Kyonki agar logon ke lunch ka hum dinner karenge, to log hamara dinner karenge, hain ki nahin?'—Since we deliver lunch boxes to the office-goers, we are very particular about time management. We cannot afford even a minute's delay. Because if we don't deliver the lunch on time, our customers will probably have us for dinner!

'Ek dabbawala gharse dabba uthaata hain, doosra woh dabba train me dalta hain, teesra station pe dabba nikalta hain, aur chautha dabbawala woh dabba lunch-time par aadmi ke saamne rakhta hain. Hamare aadmi badalte hain. Lekin khane ka dabba kabhi nahi badalta. Ek ka khana doosre ne khaya, aisa kabhi bhi nahi hota.'—We follow a relay system, where one dabbawala picks up the tiffin box, another loads it into the train, a third one unloads it and a fourth dabbawala delivers it to the customer. Our dabbawalas change but the tiffin boxes don't. There is never a case of the wrong tiffin box reaching a customer.

'Log hamain poochte hain, aap log computer kyon nahi lete? Arre, hum computer kyon le? Hamara computer to hamesha hamare saath me rehta hain. Kabhi bighadta nahi hain, kabhi kharab nahi hota. Uske upar sirf yeh cover dal do'—People ask us why we don't use computers. Why should we? We carry our computers with us always. Our computers never break down, never go wrong. All we need to do is cover it with . . . this!

When he had stood up to speak, Talekar had kept his Gandhi cap in his pocket. Now, he took it out with a flourish and placed it on his head. The audience, as expected was thrilled and clapped loudly. '. . . Bas. Hamara computer baarish me, dhoop me, chaubis ghante kaam karne ko, ho gaya tayaar!'—Our computer functions as efficiently, throughout the day, in all kinds of weather.

'Dabbewalon ke sau saal se zyaada baras ke itihas me strike

kabhi nahi hua. Poocho kyon? Kyonki dabbewale anadi zaroor hai, lekin woh jaante hain ki kaam bandh hone se khaana bhi bandh hoga!'—In the past hundred years, there has never been a strike in our profession. Because even though the dabbawalas are illiterate, they know that no work means no income and thus no food!

Pointing to his chain, 'Ham sab ne Vithoba ki mala pahni hai. Yeh mala pehenneke baad, hum daaru, cigarette, mutton, macchi kisi ko nahi choote. Haan, ham me koi log hain, jo chori chupe, kabhi kabar yeh gandey kaam karte hain. Lekin agar who aisa koi ganda kaam, kaamke time pe karte hain, to unko kadi sazaa milti hain. Hamara apna special court hain. Idhar hum log tarikh nahi dete, seedha nikal dete hain!'— Most of us wear this holy chain around the neck. We don't smoke, drink alcohol or eat meat. There are a few who do these things on the sly but if they are caught doing these things during working hours, they are severely punished. We have our own court, where we don't set the next date for the hearing, we directly mete out the punishment.

The saga of the dabbawalas, which had so captivated the audience, came to an end with another humorous anecdote about the dabbawalas. Talekar related, 'Ek pati-patni ka jor se zhagda hua. Pati bola, "maine chaalis baras tumhare saath kaise guzaare maalum nahi. Lekin ab aur seh nahi sakta. Mai jaake aatmahatya karta hun." (Once, a husband and wife were quarrelling. The husband said, 'I have put up with you for 40 years but I cannot take it anymore. I am going to commit suicide.')

'Patni bhi gusse main thi. Boli, "bala talegi, jaldi jao."

(The wife in an irritated tone replied, "Good riddance. Go quickly!")

'Pati darwaaze me hi khada raha. Patni ne poocha, "kya hua?" (The husband continued to stand in the doorway so the wife asked him what the matter was.)

'Woh bola, "meri aakhri khwaaish poori karna. Mera khaneka dabba tayaar karke dabbewale ke saath bhejna, har roz ki tarah." (Please honour this last wish of mine, prepare my lunch box as usual and send it with the dabbawala.)

'Patni ne poocha, "Kyon?" (The wife asked, 'Why?')

'Pati bola, "Kyonki main rail ki patri par sir rakh kar train ki rah dekhnewala hun. Lekin train late ho gayi to? Main bhukh se marna nahi chahta. Dabba khake marunga!" (The husband said, "Because I am going to lie down on the railway tracks and wait for the train to arrive. But what if the train is late? I don't want to die of hunger. I will eat my lunch and then die!")

Talekar concluded his speech to the sound of thunderous applause and sat down.

Now, Raghunath Medge stood up to address the audience. The auditorium lights were dimmed. A CD started playing on the laptop and these letters in English were projected onto the screen at the back of the stage, 'The wonder of dabbawalas unfolded!'

The spectators were watching the screen with bated breath because now the secret behind the dabbawalas success was about to be revealed. I admired the astuteness of the dabbawalas. They had followed the pattern of the traditional Kirtankars of Maharashtra, who started their sessions with songs which attracted the attention of the audience and then when the audience was totally receptive, began the real discourse. Talekar, with his earthy wit and sense of humour had initiated the audience into the world of the dabbawalas and now they were about to give the audience specific details and figures about their profession.

The presentation began by explaining that NMTBSA stands for Nutan Mumbai Tiffin Box Suppliers' Association. Other information about the dabbawalas was projected in brief, in English, on the screen. Raghunath Medge elaborated on each detail and gave additional information in Hindi,

Number of dabbawalas	5,000
Average education	8th Grade in high school
Area covered	Approximately 60 kms
Number of tiffins transported daily	2 lakhs
Time taken (only to deliver the tiffin)	3 hours
Error rate (possibility of error)	1 in every 60 lakh transactions
Rating given for work by Six Sigma	99.999999
Annual turnover	Approximately Rs 70 crores

Every detail being flashed on screen was followed by a thunderous round of applause. In fact, I gave up trying to count how many times the audience clapped.

Raghunath Medge explained, 'Each team has a team leader. Some are regular employees and some are substitute workers. The substitute workers are present every day and accompany the tiffin box throughout its journey. That is why, even if unforeseen circumstances arise, the tiffin still reaches the client on time. Our main objective is that the client should get fresh, home-cooked food within three hours, at his workplace. There are several reasons for our success.

'Ours is one of the rare professions in this world in which there is:

No	technology
No	fuel
No	investment
No	dispute
No	strike
No	RTO rules and regulations

There are so many "nos" in our profession. There is however one big "yes", and that is our client's 100 per cent satisfaction.

'Our profession is also unique in certain other aspects; I proudly claim that it is the most environment-friendly profession. Now let us take the example of "shareholding". We do not have any printed shares, so there is no wastage of paper. At the same time, we are all shareholders in the true sense of the term because our profits are equally divided among all of us.

'And now we come to another aspect of our business which seems to fascinate everyone; the symbols used to mark the tiffins. There have been several changes during the past 125 years in the coding system used to identify the tiffins. Initially, coloured threads were used to distinguish the tiffins, later shapes like triangles and circles or horizontal and vertical lines were used. This was followed by the use of letters in the Devanagari script but today, we use letters of the English alphabet, English numbers and a colour-coding system to identify the tiffins. Our dabbawala, who has studied on an average only up to eighth grade can read these English alphabets and all of us can decode the symbols to understand the origin and destination of every tiffin. A particular colour is accorded to every group in every area. So for example, green indicates the Medge group in Vile Parle and yellow indicates the Chaudhary group. But the colour indicates only the origin, or the place from where the tiffin is picked up. The rest of the symbols are common for the entire Mumbai city. Let us see how to decode the symbols:

'These symbols are green so it means that a dabbawala from the Medge group will pick up the tiffin.

E—Hanuman Road

VLP—Vile Parle

3—Churchgate

9E12—9 indicates that dabbawala number Nine will pick up this tiffin at Churchgate station, E indicates that it has to be delivered to the Express Towers building and 12 indicates the floor on which the office is located.

'We have allocated numbers one to ten for Churchgate. Now let us take another example of area number three in Churchgate, which is Nariman Point:

'This tiffin is picked up from an area which had been given

the code D in Ghatkopar. The destination of this tiffin is number 13, which is Grant Road. So this tiffin will travel from Ghatkopar to Dadar by the Central Railway line and then at Dadar, it will be taken to the Western Railway platform. From Dadar, it will reach Grant Road station by the Western Railway line. At Grant Road station, thousands of tiffins will be quickly sorted and from there Dabbawala number Two will take it to building P, which stands for the Panchratna building and deliver it to the customer in his office, which is on the ninth floor. Even though this system may seem confusing and complicated, in reality it is not so.

'Our dabbawala, who has been rigorously trained does all this without any problem or mistake. But there are two essential rules which have to be scrupulously followed: discipline and time management. At the very beginning, the client is given the time at which the tiffin has to be ready. The dabbawala is punctual about picking up the tiffin and we expect the same punctuality from the clients. We do our work conscientiously, the clients cooperate and that is how we win the praise and appreciation of so many people. What else do we want?'

The dabbawalas' lecture-demonstration was followed by a tea-break. I observed that while there was a large circle of people around the Medge-Talekar duo; some were praising them, some were asking them questions, everyone was eager to know more about them; Prof Dr Mani sat by himself sipping a cup of tea. And at that moment I understood the difference between bookish knowledge and real-life success in business.

24

Disputes, Fights and Other Problems

A few days ago, a reputed English daily newspaper carried an article along with photos; the heading was: 'Dabbawalas arrested for beating up passenger and stealing gold chain!' According to the article, Subhashchandra Mishra arrived at VT station just as a train bound for Thane was leaving the platform. He managed to get into the running train. The coach he had boarded was the luggage van. While he was trying to get into the train, Mishra had clutched on to the door, which slid and hurt a dabbawala, who was standing by the door. The dabbawala swore at Mishra, who slapped the dabbawala. It soon turned into a brawl, with fisticuffs flying. Three dabbawalas got together and beat up Mishra.

After alighting from the train at Masjid Bunder station, Mishra lodged a complaint with the Railway Police in which he stated that the dabbawalas beat him up and snatched his gold chain worth Rs 4,500. He also added that they tried to push him out of the moving train. The Railway Police detained two dabbawalas, Chandrakant Gaikwad and Dnyanesh Kharpude, but the police concluded that the dabbawalas did not act on purpose and they did not have any intention of stealing the gold chain.

The article was accompanied by a photograph of Mishra, nursing a bandaged hand.

Until now, only articles praising the dabbawalas had been published. This article brought out another facet of their personality. Hence, I talked to Mr Medge about this issue.

He said, 'The dabbawalas do fight, sometimes in the luggage compartments of trains and in other places. Such incidents do take place occasionally, not very often. But there is a reason for this. First, passengers often get into the luggage compartment to escape the rush in the other coaches. This is not right. Sometimes, their feet touch the tiffins or at times, they step on the tiffins while trying to get in. This infuriates the dabbawalas.

'"Why did you touch the food with your feet?"' The fight usually begins with this. The passenger is in a hurry but the dabbawala is in an even greater hurry because while the passenger only has to get down himself, the dabbawala has to get down with a heavy crate full of tiffins and also load and unload hundreds of tiffins in the matter of a few seconds. In such a charged atmosphere, it takes one tiny spark to start a fight. Another reason for a fight is that some passengers stand near the door in order to get some air. But the dabbawalas have no patience with such people because they have to start loading, unloading the tiffins the moment the train comes into the station. At such times, the dabbawala gets angry, shouts and swears. If the passenger too is hot-headed, a fight starts right then. We keep on counselling the dabbawalas to stay calm, maintain their cool and explain their problems to the passengers ... Most of the times, our advice has the desired effect and the dabbawalas and passengers try and understand each other. But they are human beings after all and hence fallible. Sometimes a fight breaks out. Even the sants, the saints, have said, "If a person doesn't listen to reason, hit him on the head with a stick." Now even if the saints could lose their patience, how can our illiterate dabbawalas be an exception? As long the dispute is restricted to words, it is alright. But the matter takes a serious turn when it becomes violent. The passenger at least has his bag but the dabbawala has no weapon to defend himself. At times, he even uses the tiffin as a weapon and hits the passenger on the head with it. This of course is followed by a police complaint and the whole rigmarole begins. The police is requested, with the help of a little incentive, to settle the matter quickly. If a policeman is a stickler for rules, he asks the dabbawala to pay a fine and a deposit. The dabbawala pays up. Usually, the matter does not go up to the court and the dabbawala too does not go back to claim his deposit. Who has the time for that? It is better to settle matters this way.

'Generally the fights between dabbawalas and the passengers are resolved then and there but if the passenger happens to be a hoodlum, matters don't end there.

'The next day he comes back with his gang members. The dabbawalas have no means of knowing even the name of such a person, but on the other hand, it is very easy to locate any particular dabbawala because he is always to be found in a particular place at a particular time. Sometimes things get out of hand and we have a tough time resolving the issue. Having said all this, I would like to add that such an incident happens once in a blue moon. See, there are 50 to 60 stations on the three different railway lines in Mumbai. There are five thousand dabbawalas who commute daily but an incident like the one you mentioned happens very rarely. And even in such a situation, where the police detain the dabbawala, his customer still gets his tiffin on time because the substitute dabbawala takes over and delivers the tiffin.'

I was impressed by this fact.

Medge continued, 'Apart from fights, there can be another problem during the rail journey; accidents. The dabbawalas are always in a tearing hurry and even though we warn them repeatedly against it, some of them cross the railway tracks to get to another platform quickly. Normally they cross the tracks adroitly but in a rare case, there is an accident. There have been cases where a dabbawala has lost a limb or even his life under the train. If such a situation does arise, we dabbawalas take care of his family. We help them financially and give/arrange work for a member of his family, be it his son or his wife and thus help them to stand on their feet.'

'I have heard that the dabbawalas also fight amongst themselves . . .'

Medge replied frankly, 'Who doesn't fight? Even brothers

stand up in arms against one another. Likewise, we dabbawalas too have our disputes and quarrels. One of the main reasons for the dispute is the accusation of 'stealing' customers. Take the example of Yeshwant. He went to his village over the weekend, which is a holiday but due to some unforeseen circumstances, he could not come back on Sunday. As he had expected to be back in time, he had not made arrangements within his group so on Monday, Yeshwant's customer had to go hungry. Some customers are understanding but Rege Madam is a strict lady. She asked the society watchman on the very same day to look out for another dabbawala. The watchman asked Govinda, another dabbawala, to pick up the tiffin from Mrs Rege's place. Govinda picked it up and delivered it on time to the customer. Now Govinda belonged to another group in the area. When Yeshwant returned after a couple of days, Govinda requested him to let him continue till the end of the month. The month stretched to two and Govinda still continued to pick up Mr Rege's tiffin. Yeshwant reminded Govinda a few times but Govinda didn't pay attention to him. Finally Yeshwant lost his temper and yelled and swore at Govinda. But Govinda insisted that Rege was his customer and nothing could change that. Yeshwant complained to his group members and Govinda did the same in his group. The two groups were at war with one another over the issue of one single tiffin. There were fights on the streets and some even turned violent. Finally the matter was brought before our internal court. The issue was: Whose client was Rege, Yeshwant's or Govinda's?

'There are no lawyers in our court, there are only judges. The plaintiff and the defendant have to plead their case themselves. After the two had been sworn in, they were asked to clarify the issue. It became clear that Govinda had acted out of turn. However, we asked Yeshwant to pay a fine, for having taken an off without informing anyone and Govinda was asked to pay double the amount for having lied. Yeshwant had to apologise to the Rege's and promise that he would not do a bunk like that again. After all this rigmarole, Yeshwant began carrying Rege's tiffin once more.

'The rules and regulations of our court are very strict. The fines are fixed depending on the offence; Rs 25 for not wearing the Gandhi cap while on duty. Sometimes the cap falls down while getting into or getting down from the train or sometimes it flies off while riding the bicycle; whatever the reason, the fine must be paid. Being absent from work without prior notice invites a fine of Rs 500; for fighting while on duty one has to pay Rs 1000; and if one drinks alcohol while at work, one has to fork out Rs 1000. As the dabbawalas know that these fines will be rigidly imposed, everyone sticks to the rules and there are very rare occasions when the rules are flaunted.

'Sometimes, there are problems with the customers. All we expect from them is to keep the tiffin ready on time. Sometimes the customers too do strange things. There was one customer, Sawant, who had two tiffin boxes. One day Mrs Sawant filled up lunch in one tiffin but the one she kept outside was the unwashed one from the previous day. That day when Mr Sawant opened his tiffin box at lunchtime, he found this empty, dirty tiffin. He lost his temper. Furious, he called up our office and complained that some dabbawala had eaten his lunch. We were dead sure no dabbawala would do that. We tried to reason with him but Mr Sawant was in no mood to listen to us. Then we made a few calls and confirmed that it was the usual dabbawala who had picked up the tiffin. What could have happened? We called up Mr Sawant's residence and spoke to his wife, who laughed and said, 'You see, it's so funny! Today, I gave the dirty, empty tiffin box to the dabbawala and kept the one I had filled at home.' She found it funny but we had spent the last few hours in tension. We called Mr Sawant and explained the matter to him. He didn't know what to say and apologised to us.

'Some customers have a habit of sending notes in the tiffin boxes, some even send cinema or theatre tickets. Some men forget their spectacles, pens, wallets or papers while leaving for office, their wives send them these things through the tiffin boxes. We don't mind it in the least. Our dabbawalas do not even open the tiffins. We come to know these things because our customers tell us about it. But once it led to quite a problematic situation . . . Mr Shah, who used to live on Nagardas Road in the suburb of Andheri kept Rs 3,000 in the tiffin box after he had finished his lunch and sent it back home. His wife needed the money urgently. It was a Saturday. Now some dabbawalas go home to their village on Saturday afternoon as it is the weekend and they have a holiday on Sunday. Shah's usual dabbawala had decided to do the same. So after having picked up and delivered the tiffin as usual, he handed it over to the substitute dabbawala who was supposed to drop it to Mr Shah's place. However, this substitute being still new on the job, couldn't find Mr Shah's house on Nagardas Road. He decided that he would take the tiffin home and hand it over to the regular dabbawala on Monday, who could then return it to Mr Shah. As soon as he reached home, he asked his wife to wash the tiffin box. This is our usual custom. Just in case a tiffin box cannot be returned for some reason on the same day, the dabbawala has to take it home, wash it and return the clean tiffin the next day. When the substitute dabbawala's wife opened the tiffin, to her great surprise, she found Rs 3,000 inside. She was tempted and without saying anything to her husband, she kept the money aside. In fact, she even spent some of it on things that she needed in the house. Mr Shah called up his wife before leaving the office and asked if she has received the money. "Money? I have not got even the tiffin box back today."

'Mr Shah was furious. He called our office and accused the dabbawala of having stolen the money. We tried to pacify him and assured him that we would look into the matter. We found out the whole story and the substitute dabbawala's address. With Mr Shah in tow, we went to the substitute's house. When we told him why we had come to see him, he started trembling and pleading, "I swear, I don't know anything about the money. I didn't even open the tiffin. I only asked my wife to wash it and keep it ready for returning on Monday."

'When we spoke to his wife, she started crying. She admitted her mistake and came back with the money. But there were only Rs 2,500 left. We apologised profusely to Mr Shah and assured him that we would get the rest of his money. But Mr Shah, who was a generous and understanding soul, magnanimously said, "It's all right. Everyone makes a mistake sometimes and gives in to temptation. Sister, please think of it as a gift for the children.'"

These stories about the dabbawalas give us an insight into their world.

25

And the Credit for the Success Goes to . . .

Whenever Raghunath Medge is asked to name the key person behind the dabbawalas' success, he modestly says, 'All of us have contributed to the success, right from Mahadu Bacche to every single dabbawala till date. Because all of us believe that work is God. It will be impossible to name all the people who are responsible for our success but there are a few outstanding people who made a significant contribution to our progress: To begin with, naturally Mahadu Bacche, then my father Dhondiba Medge, other capable members during my father's time like Prabhakar Nanaji Bhayye, Sonu Kanu Phapale, Sitaram Indore, Ganpath Ukirde, Kisan Karbhari Vaidya and many more . . . These were all forceful personalities. We had their ideal to follow and that is why we could achieve so much. Then there are my colleagues who have made such an invaluable contribution: my cousin, Sabaji

Medge, Sopanrao Mare, Damodar Pingle, Ramchandra Sathe, Gangaram Talekar and others.'

If one asks the dabbawalas the question, 'According to you who is responsible for the success and enviable reputation of the dabbawalas today?', the answer is invariably the same: Mahadu Hauji Bacche, Dhondiba Medge and Raghunath Medge!

I spoke to several dabbawalas on this subject and asked them their opinion. The general consensus was: 'Our growth, our efficient work culture is all thanks to these three presidents of our association but we would like to give more credit to Mr Raghunath Medge. He is the one who educated us illiterate people, modernised our business and took our profession to these heights of success. Before him, who paid us any attention? In fact, we were about to be ruined in the 1990s. It was Raghunath Medge who pulled us out of that situation, resolved our internal disputes and created a sense of unity amongst us. It is only due to him that we can hold our head high today and proudly say that we are dabbawalas.'

Every dabbawala's story is unique and worth learning. However, in order to understand a dabbawala's life in a broader perspective, let us meet a few dabbawalas:

This is the story of Ramu Dhondu Shinde. Shinde is the living example of the incredible amount of sheer hard work that a man can do for a living. This man has been carrying 30 to 40 tiffin boxes for the last 50 years! After collecting the tiffins from Jogeshwari, he takes them to Vile Parle. From there, he gets into the train with a heavy crate on his head and goes to Churchgate. He delivers the tiffins in Churchgate and then returns with the empty tiffins to Jogeshwari. Not only does he carry a heavy load of 70-75 kgs on his head, he delivers all the tiffins and covers a distance of around 25 kms daily on foot. Compared to the other dabbawalas, Shinde has a much more back-breaking job because he never learnt to ride the bicycle. The other dabbawalas collect the tiffins and deliver them from one place to another, using the bicycle. Shinde prefers to do the same job on foot. Just as Shinde is the only dabbawala who does not use the bicycle, he is also the only one left who still wears the traditional dhoti and long kurta. It indicates his reluctance to accept any kind of change. It was his decision to not use the cycle or to continue to wear the dhoti. Similarly, it was his own decision not to go to school. Hence, if he is asked his age, he cannot give a precise answer and it is left to us to do the mathematics. He started his career at the age of 15 and has worked for the last 50 years. That would indicate that he is approximately 65 years old. But even after spending such a long time doing this laborious work, he is as fit as a horse and always on the go. If we think about the amount of hard work that he has put in, we are stunned. When I asked Shinde, 'Do you know how to read and write?' he replied, 'Sister, I am still "angootha chaap". I can't even sign my name. But I can read the letters of the English alphabet that are necessary for me to deliver the tiffins, I can read the names of roads and streets, I can read the names of buildings, and all the numbers in Marathi and English. I can find any address in Mumbai.' It is amazing when one considers the fact that Shinde cannot even pronounce some names like 'Central Bank', which he calls,

'Santri'. But he unerringly delivers the correct tiffin to a particular office on the fourth floor of the 'Santri' building!

Shinde was voluble in his praise of Raghunath Medge, 'Till Dhondiba Medge's time, we used shapes and colours to identify the tiffins. Then this young college-going boy, Raghu said, "We should use letters which will be understood by all. First we will use Marathi letters and then English alphabets. If we use the same symbols for tiffins all over Mumbai, our system will be more accurate." You know, I was the first person to oppose him. I fought a lot against it. I said, "Who has the time to do all these new thing that this boy suggests? We don't want to change, to learn the letters. If we cannot make head nor tail of the letters, our customers will go hungry." But this boy was sure of what he was doing and his father too had full confidence in him. So then, what else could we do? We started our adult education classes, cribbing and complaining all the time. Every evening, we would go with our slates and pencils, learn the alphabet from this chit of a boy and curse our luck. But today, I admit it, we were wrong. Raghu was right. It is really great that he took all we illiterate people along with him and made so much of progress.'

There is another amazing incident where Shinde narrowly missed an accident which could have cost him his life.

The dabbawala is often tempted to cross the railway tracks, instead of climbing up the overhead footbridge with such a heavy load on his head. It saves so much of time and energy! But of course, it entails a big risk.

Shinde was used to taking this shortcut and crossing the

railway tracks. Since he had been doing this for a long time, he considered himself practically an expert at it. But then, one day . . .

Shinde, carrying a crate with 40 tiffins on his head took stock of the situation. The train was still some distance away. So he quickly crossed one railway track. He put one foot forward to cross the next track . . . and to his horror saw a train coming down on that track! In that instant, he saw what would happen; the two trains would go thundering down the two tracks and he would be caught in the middle. In a split second. Shinde turned the crate around. The trains roared past, Shinde in the middle standing with the crate pointing in a direction parallel to the trains. Shinde was saved that day, thanks to his presence of mind and his quick reflexes. As the trains rushed past, the accompanying gusts of wind were so strong that the crate was thrown against the trains and crushed to smithereens.

After a few seconds, when the trains had disappeared in the distance, the passengers waiting on the platform could not believe their eyes. Shinde was standing in between the two tracks, clutching his head, but perfectly safe and sound. He got away without a scratch, it was the crate and the tiffins which were destroyed and which he had to pay for later.

After listening to this harrowing tale, I asked Shinde, 'So, I hope you stopped crossing the tracks after that terrible experience!'

The silence that followed spoke volumes!

Dhondu Kondaji Chaudhary is another veteran dabbawala with a fascinating story. He too did not go to school and tended cattle and helped with the farming until the age of 18. His father and brother used to work in the port in Mumbai. So he too joined them. As he was not educated, he had trouble finding work. Finally he found work doing odd-jobs in a furniture shop with a salary of Rs 80 per month. As he settled down in the new city, he started meeting people and learning of new opportunities. Some of the men from his village were working as dabbawalas. From them he found out that if one could buy a 'line' of tiffins and become a mukadam, one could earn a lot of money.

So he borrowed Rs 20,000 from some employees of the furniture shop and bought four 'bakas' or in other words, he became the owner of 160 tiffins.

Now, after paying his employees and his loan instalments, he used to be left with Rs 500. This was a considered a tidy sum in those days. Soon, he became one of the important mukadams among the dabbawalas.

He bought agricultural land back in his village and arranged for irrigation and electrical connections in the fields and in the house. He got seven of his brothers and four cousins married and took on the responsibility of the expenses for these marriages. It is worth noting that Chaudhary who fulfilled these responsibilities to his family so diligently, also married four times. This was quite a common custom amongst the wealthy mukadams in those days.

I asked 'Four marriages? Four wives?' Chaudhary heard the note of surprise in my questions and clarified a little self-consciously, 'Not at the same time, Madam. One wife passed away, one ran away and one went in for a separation. The fourth wife is still with me and we have two children.'

Now that the mukadam-employees system is redundant, many dabbawalas are shareholders along with Chaudhary in this business. Chaudhary's monthly income at present is approximately Rs 5000. He lives in a room in a slum near the Link Road in Goregaon, a suburb of Mumbai. His wife works as a helper in a nursery school in order to contribute to the family income.

Chaudhary, who has never set foot in the school, is able to read and write. 'I read the paper every day. What more do I need?'

When he saw the disbelief on my face, he picked up a newspaper which was next to him and started reading slowly but clearly, 'Grand exhibition and sale of books . . .'

Chaudhary has worked under Dhondiba Medge's guidance and he cannot forget his impressive personality. He said, 'Dhondiba used his strength to keep the dabbawalas in control and in awe of him, while Raghunath uses his brains to do the same thing. Whatever the means, it is this control which is necessary . . .'

'I will tell you an anecdote about Dhondiba. Once, there was a fraud in the association's office. The person who was in charge of the accounts, sold some old water tanks and kept the money himself. When Dhondiba found about this, he formed a committee to look into the matter. The committee got all the proof required but the person would not budge from his stand and continued to say that he was innocent. Then in front of everyone, Dhondiba took up the stick that was lying in a corner and thrashed the accountant, who started pleading and immediately confessed his crime.'

Like Chaudhary, another senior and experienced dabbawala is Mr Sopanrao Mare.

While talking about the discipline in the dabbawalas' association, Mare said, 'The way of enforcing discipline was different during Dhondiba's time. It is different now. In those days, we used to keep a stick especially for that purpose in our office in Dadar. If one did something wrong, one got a stiff beating. Now instead of the stick, we use something else to enforce discipline. Our tradition of holding our court once every fortnight continues even today. There is a big picture of the two saints Dnyaneshwar and Tukaram in our office. We place the accused before this picture. We tell him, "Whatever you have to say, please say it to these two holy men. Remember, it is in your interest to tell the truth otherwise, you will have to bear the consequences of your lies." Even someone who has been lying cannot bring himself to do so when he is looking straight into the eyes of these two great saints. 99 per cent of the people tell the truth and they are then fined according to the crime that they have committed. See Madam, 90 per cent of our dabbawalas wear the sacred chain and are true followers of Sant Dnyaneshwar and Sant Tukaram. They are very scared to tell a lie in front of them.'

Sopanrao Mare has worked as the deputy president and the president of the association. He had the honour of being present for Prince Charles's wedding in London. But he still lives in a chawl in the far off suburb of Dahisar. He has started a grocery store in the chawl in order to supplement his income. His wife manages the grocery store.

Mare, who has been working in the dabbawala profession for the last 25 years, takes off his Gandhi cap and pointing to his bald head, proudly says, 'I have gone bald carrying heavy loads of tiffin boxes on my head but I am still strong physically and mentally. We dabbawalas are never afraid of hard work.'

80 per cent of the dabbawalas are illiterate as of today, others have studied up to seventh or eighth grade, there are very few who are matriculate pass or failed. There is only one single graduate amongst them, Mr Raghunath Medge.

Raghunath Medge says, 'A few children of the dabbawalas, like me, studied further. Some did their BA or BCom. Some are even MCom or double graduates. But these children did not choose to be dabbawalas. Some went abroad. Bhayye, a dabbawala, has a son who completed his MCom. This son conducts commerce coaching classes in Ghatkopar. His wife is also a professor in a college. Kisan Vaidya's one son is a professor while the other is a teacher. Some children who graduated work in banks or the Police Department or are employed in big firms. We are very proud or their achievements . . .'

Speaking of the financial condition or the standard of living of the dabbawalas, even today the average dabbawala lives in slums or chawls. If his family is with him, he either buys or rents a room. Those whose family is back in the village live 25 or 30 in a room. All they own in Mumbai is their bedding and a suitcase with their clothes . . .

Many do some other jobs to supplement their income— washing cars, delivering milk or newspapers, gardening, driving rickshaws or taxis, etc. The women too work as cooks or kitchen help . . .

Every dabbawala earns in Mumbai but he dreams of building a house back home in his village. He is ready to toil unceasingly in order to achieve that dream. The dabbawala who lives in a single room in a slum or chawl in Mumbai or shares the room with several others is often the proud owner of a nice house, farms and cattle back in his village. What else does a man need to be happy?

26

The Uncommon Saga of the Common Man

Even after Prince Charles returned to England he did not forget the dabbawalas. He wrote them a letter on his personal letterhead, 'I will always remember your hospitality. I will always treasure your gifts, the woollen shawl and your trademark "Dabbawala hat".'

The dabbawalas were naturally thrilled to receive this letter. They thought that would be the end of the story but a few months later, they received an invitation!

The prince was so impressed by the dabbawalas and their work that he used to talk about them often to the people he met. The listeners would be amazed by the dabbawalas' story and would express a desire to meet them too.

This was how the Committee of the International Food Festival which was to be held in Italy decided to invite the dabbawalas. They contacted Dr Vandana Shiva, who then conveyed their invitation to the dabbawalas. Three dabbawalas, who had never set foot beyond Mumbai, Pune or Maval went to Italy to attend the International Food Festival.

They were warmly received there. Everyone was eager to learn about their work and their life. The three dabbawalas returned to Mumbai after this successful first tour abroad. Now they could proudly claim to be 'foreign returned'.

With time, the friendship between the dabbawalas and Prince Charles continued to grow. The media too was always eager to cash in on the popularity of the dabbawalas and consequently they were often in the news. The clever dabbawalas knew they could only benefit by this publicity so they were content to be in the limelight.

A few days ago, Standard Chartered Bank was organising a marathon in Mumbai. This was an important event indeed with Sachin Tendulkar, Anil Ambani as well as several film stars participating. There was a lot of coverage in the press as a run-up to the marathon. Every day there were articles about who was practising to run and how, which star would wear which designer outfit, etc.

Among these articles, there was also one published along with photographs, 'Mumbai's Dabbawalas to Run in the Marathon.' The very fact that the dabbawalas were included in the page 3 set-up is eloquent and confirms the dabbawalas' popularity.

The article carried a detailed interview with Mr Medge who said, 'We dabbawalas do not need to practise for the marathon. We are used to running throughout the year on the streets of Mumbai. As for our dress, we will wear our uniform and run in the marathon: kurta–pyjama, Gandhi cap and Kolhapuri chappal. We wore the same clothes even when we met the Prince of Wales. Why should we change now?'

Just as news about the marathon had died down, it was announced that Prince Charles was going to marry Camilla on 8 April. This was followed by the news about the dabbawalas' preparations for the wedding. There was an article about how the impending wedding had created enthusiasm among the dabbawalas.

The dabbawalas were contemplating what gift they should offer to this 'friend' who had been the first to acknowledge and praise their efforts. Finally they called a meeting to discuss the matter and it was decided that the gifts should reflect their traditional Marathi culture. They started collecting a voluntary contribution from the members of the NMTBSA. Some gave Rs 10 while others gave Rs 25. It was decided that they would buy a traditional wedding sari for Sister Camilla and a 'pheta' or a turban for Prince Charles.

The dabbawalas and their gift caught the attention of the media and there was virtually a deluge in the press on this issue. There was at least one article a day, not only in the Marathi newspapers but also in Hindi, Gujarati and English newspapers about the dabbawalas.

'Which sari are the dabbawalas buying for Sister Camilla? Will it be a Paithani sari or a Dharwadi or a Belgaumi or Puneri sari?'

'Where will they buy the sari? In Girgaum or Dadar?'

'Are the dabbawalas going to ask their wives to help them choose a sari?'

'The dabbawalas to offer a traditional turban, "pheta", to Prince Charles! But the turban is just a piece of cloth! Who will tie it on for Prince Charles?'

'Will the dabbawalas go in for a ready-made turban?'

These headlines illustrate the obsession that the media had for anything and everything to do with the dabbawalas in those days. Prince Charles's wedding and the dabbawalas' gift got almost as much coverage as any important international news. And with every article published, there were photos of the dabbawalas, a photo of the dabbawalas choosing the sari, another photo showing them with the sari in their hands . . . Every newspaper was competing to publish the latest in this saga of the friendship between the Prince and the 'pauper', or Krishna and Sudama.

The dabbawalas did not mind all the attention in the least. After all, it was not them who were running after publicity.

After the debate regarding the choice of gifts, there was a series of articles describing in detail the gifts that were bought finally by the dabbawalas.

'Shopping completed 20 days before the wedding!'

'A bright green Paithani bought for Sister Camilla!'

'A saffron ready-made turban chosen for the Prince!'

'Kolhapuri chappals selected!'

These gifts were packed but not before they had been photographed umpteen number of times with the dabbawalas!

But the media's love affair with the dabbawalas had still not come to an end. There were still more juicy titbits to offer to the public. Articles about the dabbawalas continued: 'The dabbawalas organise a special Satyanarayana puja at the Sanyasashram to offer their blessings and best wishes to Prince Charles.'

'Gifts sent by courier to London'

Now that the topic of the gifts for the wedding had been exhausted, what more could they write about the dabbawalas?

Luckily Richard Branson came to Mumbai around this time. Branson, business tycoon, chairman of Virgin Atlantic Airways was extremely fascinated by the work of the dabbawalas and like Prince Charles, he too met the dabbawalas at Churchgate station. He too had to fit in with their schedule, since their timing was too precise to permit any flexibility. 'If Mohammed does not go to the mountain then the mountain must go to Mohammed!'

Richard Branson arrived at Churchgate station with a huge possè of press reporters and photographers.

None of the dabbawalas, not even Raghunath Medge had any idea of what a big man Branson was. Even he was a little dazed by all the attention that Branson attracted. Branson was attired in a blue kurta and pyjama. He spoke freely and informally to the dabbawalas. He asked them questions about their work, their life, praised their excellent work ethics. He even wore a Gandhi cap that a dabbawala offered him and posed for photographs with them. Then he got into a local train with them and travelled with them in the local train. Naturally the Press had a field day reporting this amazing meeting of the titans.

1 April 2005. This was the day the dabbawalas received an

invitation to attend Prince Charles's wedding and it was on the very same day that they met Richard Branson!

The attention of the media had shifted from Prince Charles's wedding and was now centred on the Branson-Dabbawala meeting. The next few days carried several articles on the subject.

A few days later, there were articles about the poor dabbawalas who had sent gifts for the royal couple but had been 'royally' ignored. The dabbawalas were busy in their travel preparations and they had not informed the Press of the invitation they had received. But some newspapers got the information.

Ironically, the very same day that Raghunath Medge and Sopanrao Mare flew to London to attend the royal wedding, the *Times of India* published a cartoon by the famous R.K. Laxman. It depicted two dabbawalas dressed in British style three-piece suits running along the streets of Mumbai, carrying their usual load of tiffins. The caption accompanying the illustration was 'What a pity! We had got these suits stitched, thinking we would be invited for the Prince's wedding! Now we will have to wear them here!' The general implication of the cartoon was, 'Oh! the poor dabbawalas!' and was also a subtle dig at the over-enthusiasm shown by the dabbawalas for Prince Charles's wedding.

But the irony was, that at the very instant that the Mumbaikars were looking at this illustration, two dabbawalas were already in the airplane on their way to the royal wedding! So, for a change, the joke this time was on the veteran cartoonist R.K.Laxman. Laxman who has accurately read the pulse of the 'common man' for such a long time was way off-target in his reading of the dabbawalas.

Because he did not recognise the fact that these 'common' men, the dabbawalas, had a strikingly 'uncommon' story!